Joe McGinniss

HEROES

A Touchstone Book
Published by Simon & Schuster Inc.

New York · London · Toronto · Sydney · Tokyo

TOUCHSTONE
Simon & Schuster Building
Rockefeller Center
1230 Avenue of the Americas
New York, New York 10020

First Touchstone Edition, 1990
Published by arrangement with the author.

TOUCHSTONE and colophon are registered trademarks
of Simon & Schuster Inc.

Manufactured in the United States of America

1   3   5   7   9   10   8   6   4   2   Pbk.

Library of Congress Cataloging in Publication Data
McGinniss, Joe.
Heroes / Joe McGinniss.—1st Touchstone ed.
p.   cm.
"A Touchstone book."
1. McGinniss, Joe.   2. Journalists—United States—Biography.
I. Title.
PN4874.M372A3   1990
070'.92—dc20
[B]   89-21945
CIP
ISBN 0-671-69511-8 Pbk.

Acknowledgment is made to the following for permission to use material:

Houghton Mifflin Company: Definition "hero" from *The American Heritage Dictionary of the English Language.* © 1969, 1970, 1971, 1973, 1975, Houghton Mifflin Company. Reprinted by permission.

W. W. Norton Company Inc.: From *Diving into the Wreck, Poems, 1971–1972* by Adrienne Rich. Copyright © 1973 by W. W. Norton & Company, Inc. Reprinted by permission.

The Philadelphia Inquirer: From columns written by Joe McGinniss.

TO GENE PRAKAPAS

HEROES

I first met Robert Kennedy in November of 1967, in Washington, just before I went to Vietnam. I was twenty-four years old and writing a column three times a week for the Philadelphia *Inquirer*. I think I was the youngest person in the country to be writing a column regularly for a major newspaper. I had been doing it for a year. Already I was bored with Philadelphia. I wanted to have some adventures.

I met Kennedy in his office at two o'clock on a bright, cold afternoon. I was there to talk to him about Vietnam, but, really, I just wanted to meet him. To have him know who I was. He was something of a hero to me then, in 1967, and I had only recently arrived at that point in my life where I was becoming aware that men who were heroes to others might someday become my friends.

Kennedy wore a blue shirt with the sleeves rolled up. He had big teeth. Behind his desk, there were cartons containing copies of his new book, *To Seek a Newer World*. What struck me most about him was how ill at ease he seemed. How much difficulty he seemed to have in talking to someone he did not know. Shyness in as public a man as Robert Kennedy seemed improbable, but there it was.

We talked—he talked, mostly—for forty-five minutes. He spoke haltingly, his voice often trailing off, his sentences often grammatically incomplete. The talk was routine, and somewhat strained, both because of his apparent shyness and because I was trying to impress him by appearing to be not trying to impress him. I learned little that would prove helpful in Vietnam, but that did not matter. What mattered was that this was *Bobby Kennedy*: talking to *me*.

As I left, he wished me luck, and, thinking briefly perhaps of what he knew of guns and bullets, said, "If you get up near, ah, areas where there's trouble, ah, be careful." I told him I would. He said, "I wouldn't want to hear that anything had happened."

Then he reached behind his desk and picked up one of the books. "Here, why don't I give you this," he said, and he inscribed it: "For Joe McGinniss, with best wishes for the future—and if you find the answer, please let me know."

I saw him again in April. By then he was running for President. It was the day after Lyndon Johnson had announced that he would not run for re-election. Kennedy was scheduled to campaign in the Philadelphia suburbs that night. There was to be a motorcade through half a dozen conservative Republican towns. I flew to New York in the afternoon so that I could come back on Kennedy's plane. It was something I tried to do whenever a politician was coming into the city from not too far away. It helped me to get a scene or two for the column which no one else from Philadelphia would have.

I ran into Jimmy Breslin at the airport. Just then, Kennedy arrived. He went straight to a VIP lounge. Breslin barged in on his heels and I followed.

"One to five," Breslin told him. "If I'm makin' book I gotta put you at one to five."

"One to five? Really?" Bobby Kennedy said.

"One to five. Absolutely."

Kennedy laughed. He seemed pleased. A few minutes later he turned to me and said, "That sounded like quite a trip you had through the Delta." I was delighted: he had remembered me. He had even read what I had written from Vietnam.

We chatted for a moment, and then it was time to go.

PHILADELPHIA—*The crowd at the airport was small, but at least it was a crowd. When George Romney came he couldn't even get a cab. There was the traditional smarty-pants question: "Would you call President Johnson's decision a profile in courage?" and then Bobby Kennedy got into the open white car and rode through the late rush-hour traffic into the lower part of Delaware County, where generations of Republicanism had gone before him. . . .*

The car turned off MacDade Boulevard and started toward Our Lady of Fatima Church, in Holmes. It made a turn in the dark and all of a sudden there were fire engines and spotlights and thousands and thousands of kids—no longer curious, staring kids but Bobby Kennedy kids, hysterical, mindless, the ones to whom he was a fifth

3

Beatle. Hero-hungry kids who cared nothing for issues, who wanted only to touch and see and scream and to feel close to something they knew was special. . . .

He could not even get to Our Lady of Fatima Church. His car had to stop at the Church of Christ, around the corner. The kids swarmed everywhere, pushing past the police, mobbing the car, reaching, bumping, tugging, screaming: mad ants overrunning a lump of sugar.

Bobby Kennedy, standing on the trunk of the car, swayed as it inched forward through the mob. One of his people clamped an arm around his waist, a safety belt to prevent the crowds from seizing and devouring him.

He spotted a face he recognized in the mob.

"Come up here," he said. "Come up in the car." And he reached out and pulled with his hand, and the police, once they were convinced he was pulling and not being pulled, parted briefly to let the new passenger on.

Bobby Kennedy was grinning, shaking his head to show that he thought it was crazy, but a mob like that puts an edge on the man who leads it: an artificial, temporary edge like two martinis, but while it is there it lifts you beyond yourself and feeds you, and Bobby Kennedy, fed by it, leaned again into the crowd, as his wife leaned out the other way, and the mad clutching continued. . . . The kids swarmed and they flung themselves at him and he rode them, as a surfer rides a wave.

Later, as his car sped up and finally outdistanced them, Bobby Kennedy sat down in the back seat. His face was alive and bright with disbelief.

"Where did they ever find that microphone for you?" Ethel Kennedy said.

He put on an overcoat for the first time. "What difference did it make?" he said. He shook his head again and grinned.

"It really matters what I tell them. They almost care." Now he started to laugh. " 'Talk about the issues, talk about the issues.' They tell me to talk about the issues." He laughed again. "Those kids really care about the issues." And Bobby Kennedy did an imitation of a crowd cheering, to show that the issues could get nowhere on this night, and I laughed again.

A few minutes later, the car got to a shopping center where he was scheduled to make a speech and I jumped out. I never saw him again.

The phone rang. I don't know what time it was. Three-thirty, quarter to four. It was my mother.

"Bobby Kennedy's been shot."

I was very sleepy. I had just gone to bed after watching him make jokes with Roger Mudd. I am not sure but I think the first thing I asked her was where.

I thought she said in the leg.

"In the leg?"

"In the head."

It was my first trip to Los Angeles. Surprising, how brown everything was. Breslin was there. We went to the hospital. We got off the elevator at the fifth floor and Breslin nodded to a guard. We walked to the middle of the corridor where Kennedy's staff and friends were waiting. They were all there, all those people who had tied their lives to his. . . .

LOS ANGELES—*They waited with enormous self-control and dignity. Nobody argued or cursed. Nobody cried. They knew he was going to die but they waited with terrible sorrow, and composure, while he made his fight. It was five in the afternoon, and already people were whispering about only a couple more hours, and the famous, efficient Kennedy staff went to work planning not a campaign any more but a funeral. . . .*

Men kept bringing in new pots of coffee, pitchers of orange juice, and muffins and sandwiches. Robert Kennedy himself was behind a set of double doors and down a corridor and around a corner; dying in a fourteen-bed ward.

"He was so happy last night," a man who had been with him was saying. "He heard early that he was going to do all right and then he kept walking up to people and saying, 'Later, we'll go over to the Factory for a drink. And tell so-and-so. I want him there. Tell him to be sure he comes with us.'

"Oh, he had it all back," this man said. "He was really going to make a run. 'I'll chase that Humphrey all over the country,' he kept saying. 'He won't be able to get away. I'll make him take a stand.' "

"The guy's a real street fighter," someone else said. "A real Irish street fighter. Imagine hanging on like this, fifteen hours after getting shot in the head."

Frank Mankiewicz, the press secretary, came out of the ward.

"Frank? How is he?"

"The same. What a heart, though. You gotta love his heart." Frank Mankiewicz made a very even, steady up-and-down motion with his hand. "Just like that. It never falters."

There was a television set in Room 533 and now it was showing the news and a lot of the Kennedy people were sitting in the room watching, and then the Los Angeles announcer said, "In case you may not have seen it Tuesday night, we are now going to show you exactly what happened at the Ambassador Hotel," and Bobby Kennedy walked into the picture with Ethel at his side and he was grinning. . . .

One by one, without saying anything, the people got up and left Room 533. But nobody turned off the television and the voice of Robert Kennedy, talking now about going to Chicago for the convention, followed them down the hall. . . .

The gray day was now becoming night, and outside in the dusk a car pulled up and the crowd screamed and ran toward it, and a few minutes later the elevator stopped at five and Jacqueline Kennedy, who had flown from Paris, stepped out, with Stephen Smith holding her arm. . . .

Later, Smith came out of the ward and said, "Probably another couple of hours." But Bobby Kennedy's heart kept going and eight p.m. became nine and ten and eleven and the fatigue was so strong in those waiting that you could smell it in the hall. . . .

At twelve before twelve, Robert Kennedy's three oldest children came down the hall and went into the ward. At twelve after twelve they came out, but ten minutes later they went in again. At twelve-thirty-five Jacqueline Kennedy came out of the ward.

"Where is Room Five-four-three?" she said.

It was at the far end of the hall—the room that had been set aside for her—and two staff men took her to it. Then everyone started to sag a bit and *people began drifting into the rooms with the beds. In 533, the television was still on, showing a movie that no one watched. George Plimpton flopped onto one of the beds and closed his eyes. His wife sat in a chair beside him. In the hall, Robert Kennedy, Jr., who was fourteen years old, walked by crying. . . .*

Then it was ten minutes of two and Pierre Salinger was in the room tapping Plimpton on the leg and nodding. Then he looked at the other bed.

"Who's over there?"

"Jerry."

Jerry Bruno, the advance man, was sleeping with his face toward the wall. He also had been advance man for John Kennedy's trip to Dallas, Texas, in November of 1963.

"I'd better tell him," Salinger said. He walked over and shook Jerry Bruno gently by the shoulder.

"It's over," he said.

Then the movie went off the television and there was a picture of Frank Mankiewicz making the announcement to the press that Robert Francis Kennedy had died at 1:44 a.m. at the age of forty-two.

But, listen: flying east, through the sadness and exhaustion, I felt pride. And a certain, possibly obscene, kind of excitement. *I had been there, on the inside, as a Kennedy had died.* It seemed the ultimate status symbol of the Sixties. And so, that June, at the age of twenty-five, I began to feel that my life had acquired new dimension.

After lunch I walked down Broadway a few blocks until I found one of those places that prints fake newspaper headlines. There was one other customer in the shop. He was about my own age and he had thick black sideburns and a heavy mustache. He had ordered fifty copies of a headline that said

WINNERS NEVER QUIT
QUITTERS NEVER WIN

He said he needed them for a sales conference. Automobile dealers, I think it was. When it was my turn I printed my message on a pad:

MCGINNISS INKS
VIKING PACT

I had six copies made, paid for them, then hurried outside to find a cab. It was a fine, bright, fall afternoon: October 25, 1972.

The contract-signing had been set for four-thirty at the office of my agent, Sterling Lord. He is from Iowa and plays tennis very well. His office is on Madison Avenue at Sixtieth Street. Normally, there is no such thing as a contract-signing; formalities are handled by mail. But I always have liked to make anything I could into an occasion.

My friend John, a banker, came up from Wall Street. Then Nancy arrived from the job she had just taken with a publisher. We went into Sterling's office and Nancy took pictures while John and Sterling and I sat on Sterling's couch and clowned around with the fake headlines and a copy of the contract. I pretended I was an All-American quarterback, just turning pro. Then I signed for real and Sterling broke out a bottle of brandy, which he kept in a drawer in case anybody who worked for him fainted. He used the brandy so seldom that he did not have any glasses and we had to drink it from coffee cups. When we were done, Sterling went back to work and John and Nancy and I walked over to Delmonico's on Park Avenue to have champagne. I ordered Dom Pérignon at $28 a bottle. We drank the first quickly and ordered another. We were talking fast and laughing a lot.

"Jesus," I said, "I feel good."

"As your banker," John said, "so do I."

Delmonico's was crowded and lively and there was music. I liked it. I liked all of it: being twenty-nine years old and in Manhattan in the fall and drinking good champagne on Park Avenue during a midweek cocktail hour with two people I was close to. Most of all, I liked knowing that a good publishing house had just given me a lot of money. It was through that sort of knowledge that I defined myself.

We drank the second bottle of champagne. John and I wanted a third but Nancy talked us out of it. "All right," I said. "Just for that we'll have martinis instead." And we did. We were happy. It felt like the fall of 1969, when *The Selling of the President* had been number one and everyone had wanted me on their shows.

We stayed at Delmonico's for two hours, maybe two and a half. Then we took a cab down to Joe and Rose's, the steak house on Forty-seventh Street. We had more martinis there, and beer, and, eventually, some steak. Then we had a couple of Irish coffees and went outside. It was after eleven o'clock and cold, with a wind picking up. I figured I had spent about $200 of the advance. John got a cab home to Brooklyn and Nancy and I walked back to our hotel.

"You know," I said, "I feel a lot better now."

"After the Irish coffee?"

"No, I mean better than I've felt in months."

"Well, you should. You've finally got a contract signed. And it's for a book you really want to do."

"I mean I feel better about us."

"Oh," Nancy said. "Is that what you mean."

"I really think things are going to be all right."

"Let's not talk about it now, love. It seems like that's all we've talked about for months."

"But I mean it. I really feel different. Everything is much clearer in my mind."

"Hurry, the light's going to turn."

We trotted across Park Avenue, heading west. At the hotel we stayed up talking very late. I told Nancy that this time I really would go through with the divorce. We fell asleep toward dawn, in each other's arms.

The phone rang. It was John. He said: "Hey, tell me again what this book is going to be about?"

"It's going to be about my search for the vanished American hero."

"I know that," he said. "But what does that mean?"

There was a pause. Then I said: "I'm not sure, John. I think it's one of those things you figure out as you go along."

Early October. Three weeks before I sign the contract. Nancy and I have been in the city. We drive home on a Friday afternoon. Larry King and a girl friend came with us. We get to the house at six o'clock, a little high still from a three-hour lunch and from the beer we have drunk in the car. The house is two hundred years old, built into the side of a hill, along a dirt road in the northwest corner of New Jersey. Nancy and I have lived there for two years. I build a fire, put on some records, pour some drinks. Then I pour more drinks and more drinks and more drinks. Larry begins to tell stories. He is from Texas and tells stories very well. He also writes them well. His *Confessions of a White Racist* had been nominated for a National Book Award in the spring of 1971. At some point, we eat dinner. Then Larry's girl friend goes to bed. She has heard the stories before. An hour later, Nancy follows. Then I start to play my Hank Williams records and Larry and I stay up until dawn. On Saturday, we nap a lot. In the afternoon

Larry and I play an adult football game that I own. He rallies in the fourth quarter to take the lead but I win with a field goal in the final seconds. There is Hank Williams again on Saturday night. We have champagne for breakfast Sunday morning. I figure if I keep drinking constantly and keep Larry with me at all times I can avoid the serious talk that Nancy wants. I play the adult football game with her after breakfast. Larry watches, and makes up dirty cheers. Larry does very funny dirty football cheers. We have the Eagles-Redskins game on television in the background. It is a Philadelphia channel and the reception is poor. Outside, the sun shines brilliantly; the air is warm and clear. Larry's girl friend has gone for a walk. We run out of champagne and switch to beer. Usually, Nancy does well at the football game but this time I am ahead 42–0 at the half. The room fills with tension like a balloon.

Nancy says she doesn't want to play the second half. I say I think she is a sore loser. Larry says he thinks it is getting to be time for him and his girl friend to start thinking about a bus back to New York. Then Nancy gets me alone.

"Why are you doing this to me?"

"What am I doing?" For weeks I have been cold and blank and indifferent. I have not fought with her, I have not screamed at her. I have not even talked to her. I have simply shrugged and turned away. It has been as if we were not living in the same bed, the same house, the same life.

"I can't stand it any more. I really can't stand it. If you're trying to make me leave, you're succeeding."

"I'm not trying to do anything."

"Do you want me to leave?"

"Do what you want."

"Do you want me to stay?"

"Like I said, do what you want."

She turns away. It is almost time to take Larry and his girl friend to the bus. After that, I am going to visit my children.

"When are you coming back?"

"Tuesday."

"Why are you staying until Tuesday?"

I shrug.

"Why aren't you coming back tomorrow night?"

"Because I'm not, that's all. I don't have to give you reasons."

There is a pause.

"I don't think I'll be here when you get back."

"Okay."

"Do you care?"

"Do what you want."

"I just can't take any more of your being this way."

"I know."

"But you don't think you're going to change?"

"I don't know what I'm going to do."

I had a theory: America no longer had national heroes as it once did because the traditional sources of heroes had dried up. The sources had dried up, I believed, because the values and ideals that traditional heroes once had personified no longer were dominant in American society. My theory was that, after a long period of erosion, they had ceased to be dominant in the 1960s.

The word "hero" was derived from the Greek *heros*, which meant "embodiment of composite ideals." By the end of the 1960s, however, there no longer seemed any such thing as a "composite ideal."

"The hero," said Sean O'Faolian, "represents . . . a socially approved norm, for representing which to the satisfaction of society, he is decorated with a title." But what were the "socially approved" norms of the 1960s? What, for that matter, was the "socially approved" society?

The poet Paul Zweig said that the hero is "an example of right behavior; the sort of man who risks his life to protect a society's values, sacrificing his personal needs for those of the community." In the 1960s, however, there no longer seemed to be an American "community," but, rather, a whole gaggle of communities, with varied and often conflicting needs.

It seemed to me that the cultural, moral and political upheavals of the Sixties, had, among other things, opened a number of new channels into which Americans, and not only young Americans, had begun to direct their quest for what was commonly referred to as "a meaningful life." Tradition, frequently bypassed—when not directly attacked—began to wither. As it did, its heroes saw their potency as symbols disappear.

A number of areas in which this seemed to have happened came to mind. Most obvious, perhaps, was the military. From the American Revolution through Korea, the military had unfailingly produced, for each conflict in which the nation was engaged, two distinct hero types: the commanding general and the common fighting man. Public eagerness, or at least willingness, to recognize these types as heroic and to pay them appropriate homage, was rooted in a tradition of the hero-as-warrior which could be traced back to Greek mythology and before. But in the 1960s, in Vietnam, the system broke down. The commanding general—Westmoreland—was seen either as a hapless victim of circumstance or as a cold-blooded killer, depending upon one's point of view, but very few perceived him as heroic. As for the common fighting man, best known was William Calley, whose exploits seemed rather too gamy to serve as the raw material of legend.

In politics, the evaporation of the Presidency as a hero-source was perhaps the most obvious example. "Potential Presidents," an adviser to Richard Nixon had written prior to the 1968 campaign, "are measured against an ideal that's a combination of leading man, God, father, hero, pope, king, with just a touch of the avenging Furies thrown in. [People] want him to be larger than life, a living legend . . . someone to be held up to their children as a model; someone to be cherished by themselves as a revered member of the family, in somewhat the same way in which peasant families pray to the icon in the corner. . . ." A few years later—not during the Sixties, but at least partially as a result of them and as a result of their effect upon Richard Nixon—the peasants had lowered their standards considerably. They no longer yearned for God in the White House—they sought simply a decent, stable man who obeyed the law.

But it was not only attitudes toward the Presidency that had changed. In 1968, there were mere contenders for the office—McCarthy, Kennedy, even George Wallace—to whose causes intelligent, caring people were willing to devote a year of their lives. By 1972, there seemed no political figure capable of holding a significant following through thirty minutes of *Meet the Press*.

In sports, another traditional breeding ground for American heroes, mythic dimension seemed lost. One could note, perhaps, the difference between the tumultuous public enthusiasm for Babe Ruth and

18

the respectful but basically disinterested attitude it maintained toward Henry Aaron as he moved inexorably toward the moment when he would surpass Ruth's greatest statistical feat. Aaron was black, of course, and possessed of a distinctly uncharismatic personality; but underlying these differences was what seemed a more central fact: the hero as home-run king was no more—due, at least in part, to television and to the overexposure of sports by television throughout the Sixties. "Every hero becomes a bore at last," Emerson said, and, with the relentless televising of seemingly endless, interchangeable, and heavily sponsored seasons, "at last" was here before we knew it.

Then there was the fantasy world of entertainment: movie stars still appeared regularly on the covers of national magazines, but who among them touched the national soul as had the titans of a generation ago? (And who among them could if there were no longer a national soul?) Among singers we had gone from Sinatra in the Forties to Presley in the Fifties to Dylan in the Sixties, but by October of 1972 we seemed to have outlived their legends. The Beatles had been magic for a time (though not American), but they were dissolved now, and their components, individuals once more, drifted restlessly from shore to shore, provoking only mild curiosity—a classic case of the sum of the parts not being able to equal the whole.

The astronauts, throughout the Sixties, were billed extensively as modern American heroes, and, at first, they seemed particularly well suited to the role. Their mission—the exploration of space—positively reeked of symbolic value. The best and bravest among us, they would carry our flag and ideals toward new and limitless horizons. But somehow the spark did not ignite. In the eight years that passed between Alan Shepard's first suborbital flight and Neil Armstrong's first step on the moon, the necessary symbiosis between hero and hero worshiper had been broken. Consider, for example, how shallow seemed the public response to Armstrong— *the first man to walk on the moon!*—when contrasted with the frenzy that had engulfed Charles Lindbergh forty-two years before.

In 1927, as a Lindbergh biographer, Kenneth A. Davis, put it, "Abruptly, across America, it was as if a hundred million minds had become one mind dominated by one emotion—and that almost a religious one. It focused on a single lonely boy . . . in a kind of passionate hope and yearning, as if Lindbergh, all alone, faced death for all of *them,* the hundred million, and by winning through would save them from a strongly felt if vaguely defined damnation."

Neil Armstrong, in October of 1972, was a teacher at the University of Cincinnati. *The first man to walk on the moon!* Teaching school in Cincinnati. And nobody cared.

Life magazine, which tried so hard to create the astronaut-hero, also did its utmost to give us the heart surgeon as hero. The possibilities at first seemed dramatic: men who moved human hearts from one body to another; men who were as gods, with the very power to give life. No wonder, in an age when mass belief in life after death had so dwindled, when life before death had become all, no wonder the wild flurry of excitement over Barnard,

Cooley and DeBakey. Unfortunately, the worship was premature: the doctors squabbled, the patients died. The human body had stubbornly refused to cooperate in the creation of what could have been a new and vital mythology. Media coverage diminished, transplants tapered off, and, eventually, *Life* itself expired, leaving its myth-making apparatus to rust away, neglected.

So. We did not have heroes any more because of the Sixties. Or because of television. Or because of the computer. Or because of the atomic bomb. We did not have heroes because of Vietnam, the spread of existentialist philosophy, the theory of relativity, the Industrial Revolution. We did not have heroes any more because of Freud. Because of Marx. Because of Darwin. Take your choice. By 1974, one would be able to say also that we did not have heroes any more because of Watergate.

The truth was, we did not have heroes any more because *there were no heroic acts left to be performed.* And even if there were, they probably would have been bad for the environment.

I got back to the house on Tuesday afternoon. It was again a very bright day. Almost all the trauma in my life, I realized, seemed to be accompanied by unusually fine weather. The house was empty. Nancy had left a note:

Tuesday morning

So. You've succeeded in driving me away. No need to name the large and horrible emotions here in the kitchen with me, but I am bewildered by your heartlessness. Don't punish me further with silence. Send a word, if only goodbye. I'll be in New Rochelle, of course. And, oh well, should your feelings change, please call. I would just like to lie with you somewhere for a few hours, just hold you and kiss your neck. Love seems so simple right now.

N.

I met her Thursday morning on Third Avenue. It was drizzling. She had come in from New Rochelle, where she had been staying with her parents. She told me she had just taken a job with a publisher. She said she would move back to the city, where she had lived before I had met her. I wanted to go to bed with her and to stay there for a very long time.

We left the city and drove up the Thruway in the rain. We got off at the Suffern exit and went to The Motel on the Mountain. It was raining so hard when we got there that it was difficult to see. We checked in at 1:00 p.m. and were given a room that looked out upon drenched autumn woods.

"All right," I said. "Get undressed."

"No," she said. "You undress me."

And I did.

Friday was chilly and bright. In late morning, we drove ninety minutes into the Catskills to my old summer camp, at which I had spent seven happy summers as a boy. But the camp had gone out of business. Cabins were slipping off their cinder-block foundations, roofs had holes, windows were broken, paint was faded and peeled. Half a totem pole lay rotting in tall grass near where the campfire ring had been. I rummaged through old papers in an unlocked staff building and found that the camp had shut down two years before. We walked slowly through the ruins. I showed Nancy cabins where my name, faded but still visible, had been written in shoe polish almost twenty years before. I showed her the waterfront, where I had learned to swim, and the lake upon which I had learned to paddle a canoe. I showed her the baseball field where one summer I had come in as a relief pitcher with the bases loaded and nobody out and had struck out the side. It was the only time in my life that I ever had struck out the side. Then we went back to the staff building and I found dozens of felt letter J's—once the highest award to which a camper could aspire—lying scattered on the floor. I picked up a handful to take with me. Then we left. I felt not only sadness; I felt fear. I decided I would have to keep Nancy with me a while longer. We drove home to New Jersey, stopping to buy a pumpkin on the way.

Of course, one might take the broader view: that there are no heroes any more because man's heroic dimension has been lost. That the hero no longer exists because, over the past four centuries, his—and man's—metaphysical underpinnings have collapsed.

"Since Copernicus," Nietzsche said, "man has been rolling from the center toward 'x.'" Throughout four hundred years of expanding knowledge and increasing self-awareness, man has seen his sense of self, of worth, of destiny, steadily dwindle—much as, in Einsteinian physics, when matter is converted into energy, its mass is reduced. The more man learned, the less he became; or, at least, the more aware he became of his own insignificance. After having spent a near-eternity tucked cosily beneath the wing of God, man found himself suddenly cast out to fend for himself—cold, frightened, and alone —in a universe that seemed not merely uncaring but totally oblivious to his existence.

And he was not even given any heroes to keep him warm. Worse, he did not know how to create them for himself. Rubbing two celebrities together did not work.

"The ancient hero," critic Victor Brombert has said, "provided a transcendental link between the contingencies of the finite and the imagined realm of the supernatural." He was, in other words, a bridge from man to God. A bridge, however, can function only between two fixed points. For thousands of years—from prehistory, in fact, through the middle ages—the points were fixed. Whatever other problems he had, man was able to maintain an essentially stable relationship with the cosmos and with his gods. There was a universe, of which man was the center, and there was a Divine Force, which controlled both that universe and man's destiny. Mysteries existed, of course—the universe itself was a mystery—but the mysteries were incorporated into a prevailing mythology that enabled man to have a sense of purpose and order about his life. He had a pretty clear idea, in other words, of who he was, where he had come from, and where he was going. His governing mythology, which, in Europe, became Christianity, not only helped him cope with his fear of the unknown but permitted him (Christianity, in fact, demanded of him) a sense of hope as to his eternal destiny. Then it was discovered that the earth was not flat. And, more alarming, that it was not fixed at the center of the universe, but that it was a sphere, constantly rotating on its axis, and at the same time, revolving around the sun. Thus, the centrifugal force which propelled man toward the terrifying unknown, and which, quite suddenly, cosmologically speaking, uprooted for all time the fixed points of man and God.

As mythologist Joseph Campbell has written, "It is not only that there is no hiding place for the gods from the searching telescope and microscope; there is no such society any more as the gods once supported. . . . The democratic ideal of the self-determining individual, the invention of the power-driven machine, and the development of the scientific method of research, have so transformed human life that the long-inherited, timeless universe of symbols has collapsed." Not only the Great American Myth—that we were the chosen people, that ours was the promised land—but the overriding Western myth of a personal God who offered personal immortality, has collapsed beneath the weight of history and has died. It proved, in the end, no sturdier than a private daydream. And its heroes have died with it. And no new myth—hence, no new hero—has yet been born.

Thus—as the broader view would have it—man today, mythless, hero-less, forced beyond the limits of illusion, sees himself as an infinitesimal and appallingly fragile part of a universe that is much bigger, colder, emptier, and more unprotected than, for millennia, he was capable of imagining. Man has been forced to realize that, if there is a meaning to life, it is not to be found "out there," in the physical world, or in the physical universe, but that it is hidden deep within the individual. And there, Campbell writes, "the meaning is absolutely unconscious. One does not know toward what one moves. One does not know by what one is propelled. The lines of communication between the conscious and the unconscious zones of the human psyche have all been cut, and we have been split in two."

The task of the searcher after heroes, then—or at least the task of him who would search after the vanished American hero—seemed primarily to be to go out and rummage through the debris of America's shattered illusions. To pick up fragments of discarded national myth, trying to determine whether anything of value—any connections—remained intact.

The task, however, was not without peril. Such a search would involve a descent into the underworld —into the darkened realm of one's own psyche— into what Norman Mailer referred to as "that rootless moral wilderness of our expanding life." Not many, in Mailer's view, were suited for such a journey. "Very few of us," he said, "know really where we have come from and to where we are going, why we do it, and if it is ever worthwhile. . . . We have lost our past, we live in that airless no man's land of the perpetual present, and so suffer doubly as we strike into the future because we have no roots by which to protect ourselves forward, or judge our trip. . . ."

The day after I signed the contract, I drove to the suburbs of Philadelphia to see my children. I had three children. The oldest was a six-year-old girl. She asked if I were going to start living with the family again in time for Christmas. I told her I did not think I ever would live with the family again. This was not the first time I had told her. It had been two and a half years since I had left. She said she was sad. And that her mother—my wife—cried a lot. I told her I knew that it was a difficult situation but that I believed that someday it would all turn out for the best. Then I told her how much I loved her: more than all the blue in the sky, more than all the red in the roses, more than all the hugs and kisses in the world.

"Yeah," she said. "You always say that, Dad. But then you always go away."

The next day, I visited my therapist. It was like being on a talk show: the important thing was to make a good impression. All I would discuss openly were my dreams. Night after night, except when very drunk, I had wild, bizarre, surreal dreams, full of anger and violence and fear. Frequently, I would dream that I was the friend of famous, powerful men: Lyndon Johnson, Ted Kennedy, Nelson Rockefeller. Politically, the dreams were nonpartisan. Once, for three nights in a row, I dreamed of Arthur Goldberg.

"Life is a journey," I said to the therapist. "I'm almost thirty and I don't feel I've even begun."

Life was a dance, the therapist told me; not a journey.

I told him I thought that was bullshit. What life really was, I said, was what Henry James had said it was: a slow, reluctant march into enemy territory.

He said he would see me the following week.

The next day, I felt sick. A chest cold. I went to bed early and stayed there the whole day. I stayed in bed also for the forty-two days after that. A local doctor told me I had pneumonia. He gave me penicillin injections twice a week and penicillin pills to take four times a day. But I knew I didn't have pneumonia. I knew that what I had was an overwhelming desire to lie in bed and be taken care of. As long as I was sick I would not have to solve problems or make decisions or act upon decisions I already had made. I would not have to get divorced, or go back to my wife, or search for the vanished American hero. Eventually, I went to a hospital. After a week they told me I did not have pneumonia and sent me home. Autumn had passed. My thirtieth birthday had come and gone. A cold wind blew through the house. I crawled onto the couch by the fireplace and waited for the year to end. *Next* year I would search for the vanished American hero. For now I would read magazines and easy novels and stay warm.

This was my routine: I would get out of bed slowly, seldom before nine. Then drive four miles to a drugstore to buy *The New York Times.* Then Nancy would make me a big breakfast. I would eat slowly and read the paper very thoroughly, attempting to justify the effort that had been required to obtain it. By the time I was finished, it would be almost eleven and the mail would arrive. With luck, there would be a magazine or two, and I could lie around, flipping through them until noon: my head still fuzzy from drinking the night before. Then I would go upstairs and pay a few bills and make a few phone calls about unimportant things. Then it would be time for lunch, after which I'd take a nap. About three, I'd sometimes go out for a walk. I would walk the dirt roads around our house and look at the cows and the bare hills and the frozen streams, and I would wonder what had gone wrong with me and would tell myself that soon everything would be all right. But if it were too cold, or too windy, or if I had drunk too much the night before, or if I just did not have the energy, I'd skip the walk. In either case, by late afternoon, I'd be settled down on the couch with a book or with more magazines. Then it would be time for a drink. At six, I'd turn on the television set and watch the news. I would watch the news for an hour and a half. And have more drinks. Big drinks. Martinis made with lots of gin. I would be cheerful for the first drink and a half, then morose. I would start to brood about my children; about the damage I had done to them; about the pain

I was causing my wife. About how disappointed in me my mother was. Sometimes I would get manic and make sudden phone calls to old friends around the country, or crazed, absurd plans for the future. Other times, for no obvious reason, I'd become enraged. I would rant and scream at Nancy, and throw things and punch the walls. The only thing that made it different from "pneumonia" was that because I was supposed to be well I would get dressed in the morning instead of staying in pajamas all day.

One day, three months later, the phone rang. The caller was a man from *The New York Times Magazine*. He wanted me to write a story about George McGovern. I said I would. Winter was almost over and my stack of firewood was almost gone. Besides, maybe George McGovern was a hero.

I looked in my dictionary. It was *The American Heritage Dictionary of the English Language*. The one with the pictures in the margins. On pages 617–18 the word "hero" was defined:

1 *In mythology and legend, a man, often born of one mortal and one divine parent, who is endowed with great courage and strength, celebrated for his bold exploits, and favored by the gods.*

2 *Any man noted for feats of courage, or nobility of purpose; especially, one who has risked or sacrificed his life:* heroes of forgotten wars.

3 *A person prominent in some event, field, period, or cause by reason of his special achievements or contributions:* the heroes of medicine.

4 *The principal male character in a novel, poem, or dramatic presentation.*
5 Informal. *Any male regarded as a potential lover or protector.*
6 Slang. *A sandwich of heroic size made with a small load of crusty bread split lengthwise, containing lettuce, condiments, and a variety of meats and cheeses. In this sense, also called "grinder," "hero sandwich," "hoagie," "sub," "submarine."*

On page 617, there were pictures of a hermaphrodite brig, of Hermes, and of a hermit crab. On page 618, there were pictures of a herring gull and of a heron. On neither page was there a picture of a hero.

I went to Washington. It was the end of March and starting to get warm. George McGovern and I walked across the Capitol lawn in the afternoon sun. It was a week when a lot of school children were around. Some of them said "Oooh!" and pointed when they saw George McGovern. He signed autographs. He was polite. He bought me coffee in the Senate dining room. He told me how much he had liked *The Selling of the President*. I thanked him. It felt good to be with a famous person again. I said our trip to South Dakota should be fun.

The story I would write would be the first big magazine story written about him since he had been beaten so badly the previous November. The purpose would be to portray the ways in which his defeat had affected him, not so much as a politician but as a person. After all, for twenty years he had dreamed of becoming President. For five years he had planned a Presidential campaign. For two years he had forced every ounce of his energies—physical, mental, emotional—into the service of that goal. The result had been the most humiliating defeat in the history of American Presidential politics. I wondered what that had done to him. I wondered how he could make himself campaign again so soon, this time in South Dakota, for re-election to the Senate.

He did not talk to me on the plane. When he got to South Dakota he made speeches. He said: "As many of you know, for many years I wanted to run for the Presidency in the worst possible way—and last year I sure did." People laughed and clapped. Then he said: "One of the problems we had last year was with our welfare-reform plan. Some people have suggested that this plan was hard to understand, so I thought that tonight I would explain some of the salient features. To begin with, everyone would receive a thousand dollars. That is, everyone who earned less than nineteen thousand, eight hundred seventy-five dollars but more than eight thousand six hundred forty-five dollars the preceding year. That is, unless more than one member of the family worked more than a hundred and five days during the year, in which case . . ." People laughed. Then he said: "We have estimated the cost of this plan very carefully, and it would range somewhere between eight hundred thousand dollars and one hundred and nine billion." People laughed. Then he said: "We took some important steps in 1972. For one thing, we made a serious effort to open the doors of the Democratic party—and as soon as we did, half the Democrats walked out." People laughed.

George McGovern had made the same speech once before. At the Gridiron Club dinner in Washington in late winter. It had been his first public appearance since his defeat. He had begun by saying, "It's a pleasure to be speaking to a friendly audience once again. And I know this audience is friendly because I can see nineteen of my twenty-three choices for Vice President here in the room." People had laughed that night, too. The way George McGovern had made fun of himself had been considered the highlight of the show. But McGovern had not remained at the dinner. He had made his speech, then left the room and hurried home.

Late one night in South Dakota, George McGovern and some of his staff arrived at a motel. "How about some fried chicken?" McGovern said. "We've got a bucket of it out in the car." I went to his room. He sipped from a glass in which vodka had been mixed with Seven-Up. I sipped vodka on the rocks. People picked pieces of cold chicken, with its congealed fat, from the bucket.

"You know what's a great drink?" McGovern said. "A really terrific drink? Vodka and orange juice. A . . . what do you call it . . . a screwdriver. That, and vodka and tonic. That's what I lived on during the campaign. Vodka and tonic and vitamin pills. I must have had four or five vodka and tonics a day. And lots of vitamins. There never was any time to sit down and eat."

"What do you take? Vitamin A? B? C?"

"All of them," George McGovern said. "I take them all."

He talked about the convention and about how he

had chosen a running mate: "Suddenly it was very late and it seemed the one guy who everybody had on their list was Eagleton. Labor was crazy about him, he was a Catholic from a border state, the blacks thought he was terrific. . . . Women said he had enormous appeal. . . . The only list he wasn't on was my own. . . . Everybody thought he was Superman.

"We did a quick check on his background and somebody said, 'Oh, yeah, he used to drink too much when he was attorney general in Missouri, but it was nothing serious.' So I said, 'All right, it's Eagleton.' He was the one guy I didn't know at all. And the funny thing is I never liked him."

"You never liked him?"

"No. Isn't that something? I didn't like him one bit. He had always seemed superficial to me. He had no dignity, no reserve. And there was always this nervousness about him. He seemed like a real Junior Chamber of Commerce type. I found out later that Abe Ribicoff felt the same way. But Abe Ribicoff wasn't up in the room with us. He probably should have been. We probably should have had a lot of those older guys around.

"The first time we heard anything at all was at a party after our acceptance speeches, about five o'clock in the morning, when Eagleton's press guy said to Mankiewicz, 'You know, he was hospitalized once for exhaustion.' And Frank said something like, 'So what's such a big deal about that? I should probably be hospitalized for exhaustion myself.'

"Then I remember a few days later, when I was out in the Black Hills supposedly taking a rest, and Frank called me from the Virgin Islands to tell me

37

about it. I was actually annoyed with him. I was irritated. I wanted to know why the hell he was bothering me with a little thing like that.

"I remember when they came to our cabin for breakfast—Eagleton and his wife—the morning we made the announcement. He was in tears, his wife was in tears—"

"They were crying?"

"Well, sobbing. Yes. I remember Eleanor putting her arm around him and telling him not to worry, that somehow everything would work out. And he looked up at me and said, 'George, I promise you one thing: you'll never have to ask me to leave this ticket. The minute it looks like I'm hurting you all you'll have to do is blink and I'll be gone.' The next thing I know I turn on the television and he's saying he's torn the word 'quit' out of his dictionary. . . ."

McGovern paused. Then he said: "To think that this guy who hadn't even campaigned for me, who had worked as hard as he could for *Muskie*. . . . That he was willing to sacrifice my campaign—"

I flew back to Washington with him the next day. He had a couple of drinks and so did I. "That business with Eagleton," he said, "That was the saddest chapter of my life. . . . What I'd worked that long and that hard for was being destroyed . . . because a guy I hardly knew . . .

He said: "That's when it hit my wife so hard. She suffered much more from all of it than I did. She was the one person who had been with me from the beginning. Who had stayed up with me all those nights as we worked, for years, to put that thing together. And then she saw it all being torn apart, by Eagleton and by the press.

"The way I felt about the press was that we blew it. I've always felt it's an adversary relationship between the politician and the press—and in the case of Eagleton they won and we lost. That's all. But my wife couldn't look at it that way. Here were all these fellows who had been dinner guests in our home. People she'd always been fond of. Who'd always seemed fond of us. And now they were doing this to me. Saying I wasn't qualified, saying I couldn't make decisions. To my wife, this was a personal betrayal.

"She'd always been a much more forgiving person than I was. She'd find an excuse for almost anyone, no matter what he'd done. But during that campaign she developed this hatred for the press, because of the way they were misrepresenting me, that became, really, a pathological thing. . . .

"It's been very rough for her since November. I've got to keep taking her out to dinner and getting her loaded all the time in order to get her mind off it. . . ."

He said: "Do you know, I almost moved to England after the election?"

"You did?"

"Yes. I was very, very tempted. And my wife really wanted to go. To get away from all of it. To leave it all behind, forever. . . . We came awfully close to going."

"What stopped you?"

"Well, I don't know. I guess there was the thought of how guilty I'd feel a few months later about having run away and left behind those two million people who'd worked for me. I guess I felt I owed it to them to stay. But it wasn't easy.

"The winter was a difficult time for me. But I'll tell you when it started to get better. After the Gridiron Club dinner. To stand up in front of all those people and make those kind of jokes about something that hurt me so much . . . My wife was very much opposed to the idea. She still is. She wishes I hadn't done it. But it was something I felt I had to do if I was going to move beyond my bitterness and self-pity. . . . I think that was the turning point. Giving that speech was a catharsis. After that, I started to feel better."

I wrote my story. I had liked George McGovern. There had been a warm good-by at the airport and a lot of quick talk about how Nancy and I would have to come down and spend a weekend in the country with Eleanor and him. I went home feeling happy that I had become such good friends with George McGovern.

When my story was published McGovern issued a statement. It said: "The article defames my wife Eleanor and friends and colleagues in the Senate, most especially Senator Eagleton." It said: "The article is full of inaccurate and fabricated quotations." It said: "In my twenty years of public service I have seldom encountered a more disreputable and shoddy piece of journalism."

Here are some things about me which possibly you should know: I was born in New York City. I was an only child. When I was five, my parents moved to a suburb called Rye. This was in 1948. We moved into a new house that my father had designed. He was in the construction specifications business. He made blueprints which architects used. His father had been an architect in Boston but had died during the influenza epidemic of 1917. My father's mother had died then, too. My father was two years old when this happened. He went to live in Wellesley with a brother and sister of his mother's. Their name was Crane. They lived together in a dark old house on Howe Street. This was the house in which my father grew up. Another uncle, Father Crane, supervised his upbringing. By the time I knew Father Crane he was Monsignor Crane, pastor of Saint Bernard's parish in West Newton, next to Wellesley. He had white hair and diabetes. He smoked cigars and drove about recklessly in a large black DeSoto. Because he was a Monsignor—in Massachusetts—he did not get tickets. He would not permit the boys of Saint Bernard's elementary school to have a basketball team because he did not believe it proper that the girls of Saint Bernard's should witness them cavorting about in what amounted to no more than their underwear. To me, Monsignor Crane was Father John. When he would come to visit, or when I would be taken to visit him in the dark and somber rectory in West Newton, I liked to run across the room and jump into his lap. My parents told me to stop, afraid it would annoy him, but as far as I could tell he did not mind. I liked sitting on Father John's lap. It was like sitting on God's lap, if God had smoked cigars.

There is this story about when Father John was dying: for thirty-five years, with skill and good fortune, he had managed the Crane family investments. Upon his death, much of the portfolio would be passed on to my father. And now, in the fall of 1952, as he lay in his rectory bed, barely conscious, the last of his life ebbing from him, he summoned my father and delivered a final patriarchal command: *"Don't sell the IBM."*

My father was made to go to MIT, where his father had gone, to prepare, as had his father, for an architectural career. He did poorly, however, and did not graduate. Then, while accompanying Father John on a transatlantic voyage, he met my mother. She was the daughter of a New York City fireman. Both her parents had come from Ireland. She worked as a secretary in Manhattan, and lived with her parents in the Forest Hills section of Queens.

She was thirteen years older than my father. They were married within a year.

My mother was forty when I was born. She had been told she could not have children, and, twice before me, she had miscarried. My birth, therefore, was considered a miraculous event. I was "Joey," her treasure, her angel, her pride and joy. Well before I reached the age of reason I was made aware that it would be almost exclusively by my words, my actions, and my fate that my mother's happiness, or lack of it, would be determined.

There were certain things which, as a child, I was not permitted to do. Either because my mother considered them too dangerous or because they did not meet my father's standards of propriety. I was not allowed to become a Boy Scout, or a paperboy, or (because it was considered an anti-Catholic organization and Father John would not approve) to play basketball at the YMCA. I spent much time alone. I read a lot. Also, I closed the door to my room and invented complicated sports games played with dice. I lived a splendid fantasy life through these games: I was quarterback, goalie, high-scoring center, brilliant rookie pitcher, champion miler. When my mother or father approached, I would hide the dice and my secret records under my bed. If they opened my door they would find me reading. Then, alone again, I would re-enter my fantasy world, feeling a surge of guilty pleasure as I closed my little hand around the dice.

We had a gardener. He came once a week to tend our half-acre. Sometimes, when he was cutting the grass beneath the windows of my room (ours was a

one-story house), he would look inside and see me
and wave hello. I did not want him to see me in my
room. My room was my private world. That a
gardener could look into it whenever he wanted
made me feel defenseless and exposed. When I
heard the lawn mower come close I would hide.
Usually beneath a counter. I would crouch there
until the lawn mower went away. I was skinny,
awkward, weak, and physically uncourageous. I was
afraid of insects, high places, the dark, barking dogs,
and hard ground balls hit right at me. I could not
help lifting my head. I also was afraid to crowd the
plate. My mother was afraid I would be kidnaped,
molested, or run over by a car. She was afraid also
that someday I would grow up and she would not
have her little Joey any more.

I wanted friends so badly I would pray for them:
please God, let so-and-so like me and be my friend.
One day, a classmate was supposed to come to my
house to play with me after school. He was late. I
began to be afraid he would not come. I was outside,
waiting. It was October, I think, or November. I
guess I was about nine years old. I walked around to
my backyard and knelt down and started to pray
that he would not call to say he was not coming. At
that moment, he arrived, walking up behind me
without my hearing him. "What are you doing?
Saying your prayers?" I jumped up—as shamed as if
the gardener had seen me playing with my dice.

I went to the Resurrection School and was taught
by the Sisters of Charity. Sundays, and on Holy
Days of Obligation, and on the first Friday of each
month, and on my birthday, and my mother's birthday, and my father's birthday, and their wedding

anniversary, and on various other days as well, I went to Mass at the Resurrection Church. That was the church where God lived, which was something the poor Presbyterians and Episcopalians, who went to the churches nearby, did not seem able to understand. God was ours. They might as well have stayed in bed on Sunday morning, and many of them did.

I said morning prayers and night prayers and prayers before and after meals. At school, there were prayers at the start of each day, in the middle, and at the end, as well as special prayers to the Blessed Virgin during May, and extra prayers for special causes, like if somebody's father was sick, or that the spread of Godless Communism be contained. I made my first Confession, at which I had nothing to confess, and my First Holy Communion, at which I wore a white suit and worried about biting the host. Communion made me feel good. It meant God was living inside me. God, who was the center of my life. I would approach the altar rail, kneel, extend my tongue, and receive the host, which was no longer merely a wafer of unleavened bread but which, through the miracle of transubstantiation (a word which I could spell in second grade) had become the actual body of Jesus Christ. Then I would rise and return slowly to my pew, head bowed and hands clasped (but pointed up toward heaven, as the nuns had taught, not down toward hell). Upon my face, I am certain, was an expression of the most fearsome solemnity. Which was as it should have been. I was, after all, filled with God, one with God, immersed in God-ness, and with not even the slightest suspicion that I would not always be that way.

I had an ardent desire to be good. Not only to

please God but to please my mother. I blessed myself with Holy Water, made the Stations of the Cross, knelt up straight, and learned how to use a missal during Mass. I memorized not only the Act of Contrition but the Morning Offering and the Apostle's Creed. I did not bear false witness against my neighbor, I loved him as myself, and I did not covet his wife. I became an altar boy, gave up candy during Lent, went to Benediction on Sunday afternoons, and confessed my little sins with regularity. I was not aware that there were any other ways of growing up.

Evenings, after dinner, my mother and father and I would kneel on the floor of our living room and say the Rosary: Joyful mysteries on Monday, Thursday, and Saturday; Sorrowful on Tuesday and Friday; Glorious on Wednesday and Sunday. Big beads, little beads, and spaces in between. I had a Guardian Angel, an immortal soul, an eternal destiny. What did it matter that I was not so happy here on earth? As long as I always was a good boy, I knew I would be happy with God in heaven for eternity.

I thought I might become a priest when I grew up. Drive a big DeSoto like Father John. I would be a kind and gentle priest and everyone would love me and respect me. I would not feel awkward and afraid any more. And I would be especially nice to skinny little boys who did not have brothers and sisters.

My father was not an active man. He was deaf in one ear, so he had not fought in the war. He did not exercise, he did not participate in any sports. Sometimes he played gin rummy. Mostly, when he was not working on specifications, or looking at his stamp collection, he lay on the couch and listened to the radio and read newspapers and magazines, and, once in a while, a detective novel. He developed a pot belly and became bald at an early age. He was a quiet man, clumsy when trying to express affection. He would put his arm around me at a football game and I'd resent it. I think that because he had not had a father to grow up with, he did not know how to be one very well. Fatherhood, I suspect, seemed to him like a second language—one that he had learned but not quite mastered.

There were times when my father did not come home. He would not come home one night and then he would not come home the next night, or the next night, and my mother would grow more and more upset and would put less and less effort into the stories she made up about where he was. Eventually, she stopped making up stories and told me the truth: he was an alcoholic. She said he would go to a store and buy liquor and take it to a hotel room and stay there drinking it until it was gone. Sometimes this required several days. Then he would call her and say he was coming home, and then he would come home and go to bed. I was not allowed to see him at these times. He would be in bed for a day and then he would get up and go to work and come home that night and come home every night for months and be gentle and kind and inactive and then one day he would not come home again. He never talked to me about it. My mother told me he was too ashamed.

Not long after Father John died, my father went into the travel business. It was something he had been wanting to do for a long time. He bought the travel agency in the Essex House Hotel on Central

Park South. He named it McGinniss Travel Service, Inc. The name was printed in gold letters on the window. It made me proud. He had matchbooks printed, and ball-point pens. McGinniss Travel Service, Inc. "Let Us Make Your Travel a Pleasure." He came home from the city with thick stacks of travel magazines and brochures under his arm, instead of rolled up blueprints. He was doing what he wanted to do. Now, he was going to be happy.

He went on television one Saint Patrick's Day. Channel 13. This was before Channel 13 became the educational station in New York. This was when it was still a seedy little station in New Jersey. Wrestling and foreign-language programs and Fairleigh-Dickinson basketball games. My father went on the special Saint Patrick's Day program to talk about the great tour to Ireland that McGinniss Travel Service was going to run. This would be a tour only for people named McGinniss. Or McGinnis. Or McGuinness. Or MacGinness. Or McInnes. Or any one of fifty or so other spellings of the name. Channel 13 came in fuzzy. It was the middle of the afternoon. Anyone else watching television was watching the parade on Channel 5. My father came on right after a Negro group that sang "My Wild Irish Rose." He seemed ill at ease, and very bald. I do not remember much else about it. In a couple of minutes he was off.

He worked on the tour to Ireland for a year. It was perhaps the major creative endeavor of his life. For a while it was very exciting. He had armbands printed up so tour members could be easily identified at airports and in lobbies of hotels. It seemed a splendid image: an army of McGinnisses, with my father in command. But not enough McGinnisses of any spelling wanted to join. A few weeks before the scheduled departure, my father had to cancel the tour and refund deposits. He talked briefly of broadening it to include anyone whose name started with Mc. Then, without saying much more, he went back to selling airplane tickets to guests of the Essex House and to people who walked in off the street.

My mother always pretended to be younger than she was. In fact, she pretended to be younger than my father. Two years younger, she said she was, and that is what I grew up believing. But her hair was gray. Nobody else's mother's hair was gray. And other mothers did not seem to cry as much or to stay in bed as much, or to spend as much time staring out the window saying nothing. My mother would not swim when she took me to the beach, she could not sleep, she was afraid to fly, and she hated to be inside a moving car. We would set out for Wellesley, or West Newton, or anywhere else, and my mother would tremble and retch and perspire. My father would keep asking her if she were having "distress." Sometimes he would stop the car at the side of the road and she would drink big swallows of club soda to bring up gas and then she would gag into her handkerchief. I would sit in the back seat and wonder if life would be more fun with different parents.

My mother drank, too. Openly for a long time, although it made her weepy and confused, and then furtively, hiding bottles in different places around the house. My father would find some of the bottles and empty them down the sink, but my mother would always manage to have another little something hidden somewhere else. She did not talk to me about her drinking. I was supposed to pretend she was normal. But she would not eat. She would not drive the car. She would not go out to buy groceries. I would come home from school and she would be sitting in a chair staring out the window. She would tell me that she "had the blues." Sometimes she would drink and sometimes not. The drinking times were worse because she talked more. She told me how important it was that I always be a good boy, and that if anything ever happened to me she would die. Without the drinking she was quiet. She would just sit and stare. Or go to her bedroom and lie down. Sometimes she would get up and fix dinner when my father came home; sometimes not. Eventually, my mother went away. My father explained that she had gone to a hospital to get happy. When she came home, he said, she would be well and would smile and laugh and would do things with us and everything would be all right.

My mother was gone for many months. Then she came home. Nothing had changed. She went away again, and came home, and went away again. An Irish woman named Sally moved into the guest room and cleaned the house and took care of me while my father was at work. In the evenings, she cooked dinner. Then she went to the guest room and closed the door and smoked cigarettes and ate oranges. She kept the windows closed all the time. The guest room reeked of oranges and cigarette smoke for weeks after Sally went away.

My father and I did not talk much during dinner. It did not seem as if there were very much to talk about. After the meal he would lie on the couch and listen to the radio and read magazines and I would go into my room and play dice games. On Sundays, we would visit my mother. She was at the Payne-Whitney Clinic in New York City. It was a very expensive place to be. She seemed sad. No one could say when she might come home. Afterward, my father and I would stop at the Carvel stand on Bruckner Boulevard in the Bronx. I ordered a toasted-coconut marshmallow sundae every week. Eventually, my mother did come home, and, eventually, I went on from Resurrection School to Archbishop Stepinac High School and then to Holy Cross College and then into the world.

Secretariat won the Kentucky Derby. Two weeks later he won the Preakness. Three weeks after that, he won the Belmont Stakes. This made him the first horse in twenty-five years to win thoroughbred racing's Triple Crown. He won the Belmont Stakes by thirty-one lengths, which is more than one hundred yards. People went crazy. I was there. After the race, CBS gave a party on the roof of Belmont Park. All over the roof, grown men were babbling, some close to tears. No one yet was able to absorb what he had seen. There seemed a sense that we, the spectators, had been, that afternoon, as near to witnessing pure greatness as it was any longer possible to be. Toward the end of the party, I fell into conversation with the CBS announcer Heywood Hale Broun. He told me that a woman had just approached him tearfully and had said that, in recent weeks, due to Watergate, rising prices, the deterioration of the environment, the specter of world starvation, and various other personal and

communal woes, she had been brought to the edge
of despair. "But this!" she had exclaimed, gesturing.
"This out here! What happened here today! *It re-
stores my faith in humanity!*"

I called Eugene McCarthy. I told him I was searching for the vanished American hero. He said he would meet me for lunch. Eugene McCarthy: for whom thousands had dropped out of school, worked without pay, given up a year of their lives. Clean for Gene. The man who had promised that government could be made decent again; who had suggested that America might again become a nation of which one need not necessarily feel ashamed. I remembered that year: the sudden wild hope—the vindictive glee, really—that sprang to life after New Hampshire. And my excitement, a few weeks later, as I sat on a dais with McCarthy in Philadelphia. Almost as thrilling as riding in an open car with Bobby Kennedy. After his speech I had walked over to the lectern and had picked up the piece of paper on which he'd made notes. *"Apocalyptic mood . . . 1968—Important Year . . . Testing of America . . . Apocalyptic Mood . . . Charisma . . . Where Were You—1968 . . . Nation of Sheep . . . Children's Crusade*

. . . *1968* . . ." I had folded the paper and taken it home and put it inside my copy of Bobby Kennedy's book. Corsages from my Junior Prom.

We ate at Toots Shor's. It was a place where McCarthy was known. I was nervous and drank martinis. There was much that I wanted to get at but did not know how. McCarthy drank manhattans. He was working as an editor at Simon & Schuster. He did not remember me from 1968. We had three drinks each before we ate.

What I wanted to say to him was: "Look. Once you were at the center of things. Everything revolved around you. You had squeezed your whole universe into a ball and had held it in your hands and no one could touch it. Now it's gone. The moment has passed. It won't be back." I wanted to say also that once I had been at the center of things: at twenty-six I had written a book which had become the best-selling nonfiction book in America. It had got good reviews almost everywhere. It was deemed important, and, as its author, so was I. The youngest person ever (I was told) to have written a book that became number one on the *New York Times* bestseller list. Not counting Anne Frank. Then the moment had passed. In many ways, as McCarthy had seemed to, I had tried to make it pass. Part of him had needed to not win. Part of me had needed to not succeed. I had moved to New Jersey. It was like going to my room and closing the door as a child. Now, I wanted to ask Eugene McCarthy, *What happens next? Where is the center of things? Why didn't we stay there? Will we ever be there again?* He would know. After all, once he had studied to be a priest.

We talked about baseball instead. I felt high on my three martinis, and then I drank beer with my lunch. McCarthy was funny, and wry, but not a man inclined' toward quick intimacy. At the end of the meal, unexpectedly, Howard Cosell arrived. He had come to film an interview with the commissioner of professional basketball. My old buddy Howard. Effusive with drink, I introduced him to McCarthy. I had written about Cosell, had traveled with him, had been interviewed by him, had stayed in his apartment for a week. His older daughter had married the younger brother of one of my closest friends from high school. I had talked with him on airplanes about such matters as life after death. Nothing seemed more obvious, now, than that the three of us should go out for drinks as soon as Cosell finished his interview. My buddy Howard and my buddy Gene. We would have a wonderful New York sort of adventure. Just drinking and laughing, shooting the breeze and feeling fine. For a few hours, at least, I could feel as if I were back at the center.

I went to the men's room. Then I called Nancy to say I would not be home for a while. But when I got back to the table McCarthy was gone. I looked in the back room where Cosell was filming. No McCarthy. I checked the bar, went back downstairs and checked the men's room: no McCarthy. Five minutes earlier, he'd been sitting at the table with me, making plans for the rest of the day. Now he was gone. Hazily, I walked back to Simon & Schuster and rode the elevator to his office. It was the same elevator I had ridden when my book was number one. Yes, Mr. McCarthy was in, but he was busy. Did I have an appointment?

"You don't understand. We just had lunch together."

Five minutes later, they let me in to see him. He did not appear to think he had done anything strange. He said he had not known where I'd gone and it had seemed a better idea to go back to the office than to wait around to go drinking with Howard Cosell. So he'd left. Clumsily, I made plans to see him again in the fall. Maybe when he was going out on a speaking tour I'd go with him. See how much of the old magic remained. Yes, yes, he said; that would be fine. The gin cloud was gone. I had a dull headache and a bad taste in my mouth. I walked to Port Authority and rode a bus home.

June, one year earlier. 1972. It starts to rain. It rains all day and all night and all day and all night and all day and all night. It rains for a week. We have a termite man in the house. He is pulling up the boards of the living-room floor, so he can dig a big hole and make tunnels through the dirt underneath. Then he will pour poison into the tunnels. Nancy and I lie upstairs on our bed and listen to him dig. It keeps raining. Nancy tells me she is leaving. She says she is going to London to live with her sister for a while. I have been trying all spring to make her do this. So I can go back to my wife and my children and get rid of my guilt. I tell her I will drive her to the airport. . . .

She left on a Friday night. There were clusters of nuns and student tour groups at the airport. I kissed her good-by. It was the first time I had kissed her in weeks. Then I drove home through the heavy rain. I drank a glass of milk and ate fudge. It was almost midnight. I read a magazine story about Groucho Marx and went to bed. The house seemed empty and still. It smelled of termite poison. The bed seemed very big. I had vivid, strong dreams about tornadoes, and woke up at five o'clock in the morning. I ate Bucwheats and blueberries for breakfast. Nancy had left the kitchen very neat. I browsed through a catalogue from a wine shop. Then I read a short story in *The New Yorker*. Then I talked to my children and my wife. I did not tell them that anything had changed. Then I paid bills, read T. S. Eliot, listened to Beethoven, did calisthenics, and ran a mile and a half. The rain had stopped but the sky remained dark. I showered. I listened to more Beethoven. I ate a dinner of olives, an orange, provolone, canned peas, and pumpernickel bread. I drank water with the meal. After dinner, I read *Memories of a Catholic Girlhood*, by Mary McCarthy. It began to rain again Saturday night. I got up at nine o'clock Sunday morning and went for the paper. It was the fourteenth consecutive day without sun. There was bad flooding in Pennsylvania and New York. Dozens were dead, thousands homeless. I ate peanut butter and bacon and drank tea. I was grateful for the floods. They made the newspaper more interesting. I called my mother. We did not find much to talk about. I did not mention that Nancy had gone away. My mother preferred to pretend that Nancy did not exist. I ate yogurt and wheat germ for lunch. I was trying to purify myself. I exercised and ran another mile and a half in midafternoon. There was a pale trace of sun in a gray sky. I finished Mary McCarthy and ate grilled cheese and bacon for supper. At 6:15 a weak sun shone through haze.

The next day I visited my children and my wife. I stayed overnight. And stayed the next day. I still did not tell them that anything had changed. Because I wasn't sure anything had. I played with the children. Then, in the evening, I started to drink. I drank martinis through dinner, then switched to Grand Marnier. My wife went to bed. I sat downstairs and kept drinking. There was a long cord on the kitchen telephone. I dialed 0, then carried the receiver to the basement. When the operator came on I gave her the number in London. Nancy's sister's apartment. It would be 3:30 a.m. London time. The phone rang. And rang some more. There was no answer. I tiptoed back to the kitchen and hung up. At midnight—5:00 a.m. London time—I tried again. Still no answer. I fell asleep on the couch. I woke up at 4:30 with my teeth chattering. I tiptoed downstairs and called again—9:30 a.m. London time. There was no answer. In the morning I called from a shopping-center pay phone, charging the call to my number in New Jersey. It was 1:30 p.m. London time. Nancy answered. I told her I wanted her to come back. I said that this time everything would be different.

Her plane was late. I sipped cold beer in a dark bar at the airport. I waited three hours before she walked through the swinging doors of the customs shed, wheeling her luggage in a cart. She was wearing an orange see-through top and bell-bottomed pants. They were new. They were exciting. We drove home through thunderstorms and heavy traffic. She touched my cheek, she kissed my neck, I touched her breasts. I told her how I loved her; told her my fantasies, my fears, and my desires.

HEROES

We got home. The house was dark. We did not turn on any lights. We left her luggage in the living room and climbed the stairs. We heard the rain falling. Then we touched. And then we heard only our longing and our love.

saw Eugene McCarthy again in the fall. He made a speech at the University of Pennsylvania. "It wasn't easy to get him booked," a student said. "Our chairman didn't want him. Felt he was washed up. We had to get up a petition." There was a press conference in a basement room beneath the auditorium where McCarthy was to speak. One professional reporter was in attendance. "Channel Ten was sending a crew," a student said. "But then a cop got shot." McCarthy said he was ready for any questions. There was a scraping of metal chairs on the stone floor of the nearly empty room. The sense was of being inside a sepulcher. The trouble was, there was not really anything to ask. Upstairs, the twelve-hundred-seat auditorium was half empty. A member of the speaker's committee shook his head. "This might have been a mistake," he said. "He hasn't even drawn as well as Shirley Chisholm."

I went with him to Washington. I went to his house in Georgetown in the morning. He lived there with one of his daughters. He was separated from his wife. It was a cold, gray morning. McCarthy wore blue jeans and blew his nose frequently. He said his feet got cold at night. He got up to put on a sweater. The phone rang. He walked stiffly toward it. His left knee hurt him in damp weather. He called to his daughter upstairs.

"Ellen? There's a call from your mother. Do you want to take it on my phone or do you want to call her back?"

His daughter took the call. He walked stiffly back to his chair. A big man; still strong. An old first baseman whose legs have started to go. He would not be sorry if today's game were rained out.

We drank coffee. And talked about 1968, when he had seemed a hero to so many. He did not object to the term. "What you had, really," he said, "was two heroes, kind of competing. Then one was killed. In a situation like that, being the survivor, you don't have a chance. Of course, McGovern kept Bobby running against me. George kept saying I had no compassion for the poor, and of course everyone knew that Bobby did." He paused. "I do, as a matter of fact. I have lots of compassion." He said he might run for President again in 1976. "I get the feeling it's coming round again. I'm picking up more of it. I'm starting to see it a lot from the airport types. 'You were right,' they keep telling me. I don't ask them what it was I was right about."

In October, I rode the late-afternoon ferry to Martha's Vineyard. I was going to visit William Styron. I had met him only once, but in Roxbury, Connecticut, during the summer of 1970, while he was away, I had played tennis often on his court. I had been renting a house around the corner. I had been twenty-seven. It had been my first summer with Nancy. The summer after my book had made it big. William Styron, because of *Lie Down in Darkness*, his first novel, had seemed a hero. The book had been published twenty years earlier, when Styron had been twenty-five. I had read it four times. It was a fine, rare, desperate book; one that scared me more the older I got. I could not imagine how Styron could have written it at twenty-five. I was coming to see him now because I wanted to know where a man could be with his life twenty years after writing such a book.

The afternoon was humid, very warm. Styron was waiting at the ramp, cordial, a bit paunchy in sweater and slacks. He was staying on alone at his summer home, trying to get a new novel under way. His wife and children had gone back to Connecticut. He said he thought a few weeks of solitude each year were good for the soul. We rode in his Jaguar, of which he was fond. "Most cars," he said, "are starting to wear out at thirty thousand miles, but this is just beginning to mellow." We picked up a girl who was hitchhiking to a karate school across the street from Styron's house. "Some days," he said, "I can hear thumps from there like distant thunder." Toward dusk, we toured the island, talking mostly of the Kennedys, of Ted Kennedy in particular, and of Chappaquiddick. Ted Kennedy was a friend of William Styron's. We paused at Edgartown and looked across the channel. Then we went back to the house and started to drink.

I drank martinis. I was talking a lot. As with McCarthy, I felt nervous. As with McCarthy, there was much that I wanted to get at but didn't know how. I wanted to talk about heroes, and illusion, and the heroic effort required to live without illusion, or beyond the boundaries of the illusions which one had been conditioned to accept. I wanted not an obvious rhetorical exchange about why America had no national heroes any more; I wanted to get at how one kept one's world from collapsing once its mythic underpinnings had given way. Beyond that, I wanted to feel a closeness to Styron, a degree of intimacy, a sense of shared experience, even though, except for the fact that from time to time each of us occupied himself with the effort of filling blank pieces of paper with words, there had been none. I wanted, mostly, to feel *accepted* by Styron, because—all contrary evidence from the past notwithstanding—I thought that might make me more acceptable to myself.

We went to dinner. Styron mixed drinks to bring along in the car. An old southern custom, he explained. An old northern custom, too, in my experience. The restaurant was expensive, pretentious, not very good. Styron said he might write a nasty article about it in the local paper. We drank a considerable amount with the meal. Then we went back to the house and drank more. We sat up talking and drinking through the night. We talked about journalism, fiction, love, politics, death, the South, the Irish, mental health, monogamy, courage, fear, gambling, drinking, children, Catholicism, country music, football, divorce, and the new book that Styron had started to write. He said the idea for it had come to him one night during a dream in which he had seen writing on a wall. So that was it: Joyce Carol Oates heard voices; William Styron saw writing on a wall in his dreams. I told him he wasn't so hot—it was just that he had a good Guardian Angel.

I drank up all his imported beer and most of his domestic. Drinking, as I'd observed in the past, reduced drastically the distance between me and whomever I was with. It was, of course, a temporary reduction, a false intimacy, and one that would be paid for when the morning revealed anew how great the distance truly was. But false intimacy, like a false god, like any other illusion that soothed and cheered, seemed preferable to the alternative, which was no intimacy, no god—no hero—no illusion at all.

Suddenly it was five-thirty in the morning. Gray light outside. My eyes stung, my throat was sore, I could feel beard stubble on my chin. Styron looked slightly puffy and red-eyed himself. He was saying, "What it all comes down to, I guess, is either you've got talent or you don't. And if you don't . . . well . . . I guess you're screwed." I nodded, said good night, and trudged upstairs to bed.

I woke up at ten-thirty, if not still drunk, then not yet quite sober. The morning was murky and wet. Styron was still sleeping. I went down to the kitchen looking for something to eat. I opened the refrigerator. The first thing I saw was the can of fresh, vacuum-packed crabmeat, which had been shipped up from Georgia. He had told me about this crabmeat in some detail the night before. It was the only canned crabmeat in America, he had said, which tasted like fresh crab. This was due to the vacuum-packing, he had explained. It was very expensive crabmeat and extremely hard to get and it was one of his favorite things to eat. He had been saving this can for a special occasion because it was the last he would be able to get until the following summer.

I opened it. It made a hissing sound, like a can of peanuts, or tennis balls. I ate a piece. It was delicious. Moving quickly to his pantry I took out some flour. Then some Tabasco, and Worcestershire sauce. Then I took eggs, milk, heavy cream, butter, and green peppers from the refrigerator. Then I made bread crumbs. I had to move fast. I had to get this done before he woke up. I mixed, rolled, measured, stirred, and poured, for twenty minutes. Then I put the whole business in the oven. It would be crabmeat pie: an original recipe. It would be delicious. How could it miss? I had used the whole big can of crabmeat.

I opened the oven door and peeked inside. It seemed to be coming along fine. I'd even remembered to butter the bottom of the Pyrex dish so that it would not stick when I took it out. Lovely aromas filled the kitchen.

I heard a creaking of bedsprings upstairs. Then the sound of water running. Then slow, heavy footsteps down the stairs. William Styron, in red bathrobe, hair mussed, face wrinkled from sleep, walked into the kitchen of his summer home on Martha's Vineyard. For a moment I do not think he remembered who I was.

"Morning, Bill."

"Nmph." He sniffed. "What do I smell?"

"Oh, just a little brunch I was making for us. It's in the oven now."

"Huh?" He opened the oven door and looked inside. It would not be ready for another ten minutes.

"What the hell is it?"

"Well, actually, it's sort of an original recipe. But basically what it comes down to is, ah, crabmeat pie."

"Oh." He walked slowly across the kitchen and looked out at the sodden day. "Did you say crabmeat?"

"Yup. Crabmeat pie."

"Where'd you get the crabmeat?"

"You had some in the refrigerator. Remember? We were talking about it last night."

"You used *that* crabmeat?"

"Right. This really ought to be delicious, Bill. And it should be ready in just a few minutes."

"You used my last can of fresh crabmeat to make *breakfast*?!"

"Well, actually, by the time we get around to eating it I suppose it will be more like brunch."

He stared at me. I think he was beginning to suspect that I was mad. "Little damp out there," I said, pointing out the window.

"What the hell did you do that for?"

"Oh, I just figured we deserved a good meal."

He walked back to the oven and opened the door. "My crabmeat," he said, watching it bubble.

"Smells great, doesn't it?"

"What the hell else did you put in this?"

"Tobasco, Worcestershire, a few spices, green pepper, some butter, breadcrumbs, heavy cream. Then your basic pie-crust mixture."

"That crabmeat has a very delicate flavor."

"I know. I sampled a little before I mixed it into the pie."

He closed the oven door and stared at me again. It was as if he had come upon me making love to his wife. "I didn't expect you to do this," he said.

"It should be delicious."

"I didn't expect this at all." He seemed now to be speaking more to himself than to me. He left the kitchen. I could hear him walking slowly back upstairs. I opened the oven. Five more minutes. It sure smelled great.

William Styron, dressed now, came back into his kitchen. "I'm going downtown," he said, putting on a raincoat. "Have a . . . a beer or something." I wondered, momentarily, whether he might be going to fetch the police. . . .

The crabmeat pie was ready when he got back. It was superb. The flavors blended perfectly, the consistency was marvelous, the crabmeat had remained moist and fresh. We ate the whole thing, along with some tomatoes that Styron had picked from his garden. We drank beer. Styron mellowed, like his Jaguar. The spirit of camaraderie was revived.

"It's really damned fine," he said. "For a while there I was afraid you didn't know what you were doing."

"I just followed my instinct."

"Damned fine."

He drove me to the ferry in the Jaguar. I felt that my trip had been worthwhile. I boarded the ferry. He waved good-by.

In November, I flew to Winnipeg, Manitoba, to visit Daniel Berrigan. It was cold and there was snow falling as I rode in from the airport. City lights glowed in the distance. The overnight temperature would go below zero, the cab driver said. He asked if I had been to Winnipeg before. Yes, I said. I had. Fourteen months earlier. I had stopped there for an hour on a train. . . .

We board in Toronto on a Sunday afternoon. The plan is this: we will get off Tuesday night at Jasper, Alberta, in the Canadian Rockies. We will hike for two weeks, then board another train for a ride through the mountains to Vancouver, then fly home. The mountains will be unlike anything we've ever seen. We will walk through them all day, growing stronger, then make contented love at night in rustic cabins. And the train ride itself, in the private drawing room I have reserved, will be a romantic adventure. . . .

"What's wrong?"

"Nothing's wrong. Why are you asking me what's wrong?"

"You just seem so remote."

"So, I seem remote. I think I'm entitled to seem remote."

"But I'm wondering why."

"Just leave me alone, would you please? I'm on vacation." So Nancy turned back to her book and I turned back to mine. The drawing room was cramped, the train noisy, the food bad, the view of Ontario's shimmering lakes dulled by dirt-streaked windows.

"Do you feel guilty? Is that it?"

"What?"

"I just wondered if you were acting this way because you felt guilty. Punishing yourself for taking this trip and punishing me for going with you."

"I'm not punishing anybody for anything."

A pause. Then: "I consider it a punishment when I see you acting this way."

"Well, that's your problem, not mine." Outside, the Manitoba prairie sped past: endless, changeless, flat as death. The train stopped at Winnipeg in the night. Sluggish, dull, unspeaking, we walked the streets for half an hour, then reboarded.

But then, late Tuesday, I saw the mountains. At first they were clouds on the horizon to the west. Half an hour later they were mountains, but toy: pieces from a child's play-village set. The train shot closer and I went to the club car, alone. There was definition now on the horizon, and, forming quickly, heightened by gin, the sense that the mountains were real. And a sense that in speeding toward them,

I, too, was suddenly becoming real. I drank more gin.

The mountains: I would plunge into them, become part of them, rise with them; and, through them, would rise above all anger, depression, and guilt. The mountains were magic. They would make me magic, too. I would need no one: not Nancy, not my wife, not my children. Better yet, no one would need me. Unbounded, I would live a rarefied mountain life, and, like the mountains, would triumph and endure. I suddenly became wildly exuberant. I felt free. I drank more gin.

Daniel Berrigan was teaching at the University of Manitoba. He had arrived in September and would leave before Christmas. He was there, he would tell me, because after the Sixties, after the war, after the fame, after the running and hiding, after two years in prison—after having been a hero to so many—he had needed a rest. He had needed time, he would say, "to clear a space away for myself."

I was there because I wondered what it was like for a hero when there was no longer anything to be heroic about. Berrigan had gone to jail for opposing the war, but the war was over. He had gone to jail for disrupting the draft, but the draft was over. He had been, as had George McGovern and Eugene McCarthy, at the center. Now, the center had dissolved, and he was in Winnipeg, Manitoba, instead.

Unless, of course, he somehow had been able to carry his own center with him. To remain the hero of his own myth, even as the American myth, the religious myth, the Resistance myth, were collapsing. Unless, in other words, he had been able to sustain a belief in his own illusions, even as he acknowledged certain facts that had destroyed those illusions for others. He had, after all, remained a priest. He still sensed, apparently, that there was something of value in that. I wondered what it was. I wondered if he knew. What was it that lived for him at the core of the myth, and how had he managed to keep it alive?

I got out of the cab at the Fort Gary Hotel, a big old hotel, across from the railroad station where the train had stopped a year before.

We reached the mountains an hour before dark. Sudden as a slide-projector click. The prairie ended. The mountains began. There were moose along streams, high hills of pine and rock, and, seen through a gin haze from the domed observation car, startling, massive, snow-covered peaks. At nine o'clock we got to Jasper, a hundred miles north of Banff and Lake Louise. We went to a cabin in the woods, at the edge of the Athabasca River, which moved swiftly, noisily, in the night. We sat on the bank, in sweaters, breathed pine air, drank red wine, looked at thousands of suddenly-accessible stars. We went to bed exhilarated, hungry for morning, craving the sight of high peaks.

And yes, we had some good days. The first: rising thirty-five hundred feet on a tram, then walking over the top of the ridge behind the tram station and hiking for two hours after that—high and free in the sunshine and the wind, with no one else in sight. We had a three-hundred-and-sixty-degree view: of peaks, thrusting like weapons at the sky; of winding river valleys far below; of green meadows and distant, amethyst lakes. For a whole afternoon we shared ecstasy. But soon I grew cold again, like the air at our new elevation. And sullen, like the sky as snow approached. Angrily, I stalked ahead, berating Nancy for her slowness, her fatigue. If I could not find joy or peace in the mountains, I would find purification through striving and pain. We no longer spoke. I walked fifty yards ahead of her, keeping her out of my vision; I did not want her interfering with the view.

Then winter came. In mid-September. Snow covered the trails, and hiking was over for the year. We flew to Vancouver Island, off the coast of British Columbia, then drove up the isolated western shore, where there were only Indians and logging camps and rain. Three hundred inches of rain a year. We found a cabin on an empty beach. There was rain forest at the edge of the beach, snow-capped peaks in the distance. We stayed for five days. It did not rain. We saw nothing but sun, stars, and pure blue sky. The days were warm, the nights cool; there were miles of deserted beach to walk, rocks to climb, forest to explore. In the evenings the sun turned red as blood. We ate giant crabs and whole steaks of locally smoked salmon. It seemed that the earth was flat, after all, and that we had reached its northwest edge. But I would not talk to Nancy, would not touch her, did not want her near me night or day. I was at the brink of rage constantly. I felt that my soul was flat, too, and that I had reached its northwest edge. Nancy represented all the wrong I had done to those to whom I was obligated to always do right: my mother, my children, my wife. She was ceaseless proof that I wasn't good little Joey any more. That was why I needed her, and that was why I tried so hard to drive her away. "How wonderful this vacation would have been," she wrote in her diary, "had we been lovers."

We flew to Seattle. I lived alone inside myself. At my core there was a fist which I kept clenched. What was inside the fist I did not know. Maybe nothing. I got drunk in Seattle and wound up on the telephone at midnight—3:00 a.m. in the east—trying to track down old friends from summer camp. People I had not seen in ten, in fifteen years. I called all over Connecticut, Long Island, Washington, D.C., waking up parents, brothers, children, wives. I felt a powerful need to talk to people who had known me before I had become the way I was. Nancy said maybe I had made enough calls, had woken up enough peaceful sleepers in the east. I screamed at her. She went to bed, sobbing, I kept on calling through the night.

Daniel Berrigan unslung a book-filled canvas knapsack from his shoulder. "Ah," he said, "the searcher after heroes has arrived."

His face was full—not gaunt, as I'd expected. He had a mustache and a wispy goatee. He seemed a bit thick through the middle. He was, I remembered, fifty-two.

"I see that Peter has welcomed you with a cup of tea, made from our communal teabag."

"Actually," Peter Jordan, his teaching assistant, said, "I gave him a fresh one."

"Oh?" Daniel Berrigan rolled his eyes.

"After all," Jordan said, "he's an American."

"Ah, yes, an American. How delightful to have an American in our midst."

I went to dinner with him at Jordan's apartment. It was in an old wooden frame building overlooking the Saskatchewan River. There was a view of downtown Winnipeg across the river. The temperature was six degrees. We ate cheese and fish and drank warm Canadian rosé. Berrigan and Jordan said "Wow" a lot, as in "Hey, great . . . wow . . ." and, "Hey, wow . . . terrific." After dinner we crossed the river to another wooden-frame house and walked up a flight of inside stairs to a second-floor apartment. There were about twenty people in a living room, waiting for Berrigan. These were the people to whom his presence in Winnipeg meant the most: students, social workers, people committed to causes. He spent an evening with them every week. They talked to him about their problems, sought his advice, basked in the glow of his aura. Then they prayed with him, and often, at the end, they shared with him the sacrament of the Eucharist.

On this evening there was, first, extended discussion of whether or not members of the group should establish a summer commune. Then there was extended discussion of whether or not three girls from Toronto who had come to Winnipeg to take Berrigan's courses should return to Toronto when he left or should stay in Winnipeg to work for the cause of migrant workers. Then there was extended discussion of the planned supermarket boycotts on behalf of the cause of migrant workers. Then there were extended discussions of ways to raise money for the cause of migrant workers. Berrigan said he might give a poetry reading to raise money. This sent ripples of excitement through the room. Then one of the girls from Toronto read aloud from her Bible. I could see that many of the passages had been underlined in colored ink. After the reading there was group discussion about the meaning of the text. "I really get excited," one of the girls from Toronto said, "when I read that prayer is the working of the spirit within me." It was agreed that her excitement was not uncalled for. Then instant coffee, tea, and cookies were served, accompanied by much murmuring of, "Hey, wow . . . terrific." Except when someone noticed that the coffee had come from Safeway, and Safeway was a store to be boycotted. That caused extended discussion about whether or not the coffee should be drunk. It was agreed, finally, that since it already had been paid for, the drinking of it would not constitute an act of disloyalty to the migrant workers. Then someone took out a guitar and singing began. Regular old folk songs, migrant-worker songs, and, at Daniel Berrigan's request, "Little Boxes," the Pete Seeger song which suggested that suburban housing developments and the people who lived in them were not where it was at.

I had a headache. The room was overheated, overcrowded, filled with smoke. And filled, too, with the kind of naïve zealotry that gave me a headache even in fresh air. I was grateful for the opportunity to have witnessed hero-worship in action, but I found that it put me in a very bad mood.

Daniel Berrigan chose not to perform a Eucharist. This was because I was there, and would be writing. The Eucharist, apparently, was what lived at the core of Berrigan's myth. He was taking no chance of having it sullied by exposure to a representative, however unorthodox, of the media. Which was fine with me. No matter how total my break with tradition, I still would have felt bad about being the only person in the room who did not receive Holy Communion.

Berrigan came to my hotel for dinner the next night. He rode in from the university on a bus. He wore ragged jeans and desert boots and an old plaid shirt under his jacket. I met him in the lobby and we went to my room to talk. He talked about having been a hero in the Sixties. He said: "The trouble is, they want to devour you. They want to consume you. They need heroes, yes—but what they *want* are hero sandwiches." He talked about his feeling for tradition. He said: "I believe there is some form of specialness involved in being a priest. I had this woman come up to me not long ago, gushing all over about how she had just attended this marvelous Eucharist performed by a 'very charismatic rabbi.' Now, what kind of bullshit is that? A 'very charismatic rabbi' performing a Eucharist. And I was supposed to think it was heart-warming. Ecumenical, you know. Man, I just can't take it with these people who are trying to make alphabet soup out of tradition." He talked about the condition of modern man. He said: "I think from any realistic point of view it's apparent that we're used up spiritually. This energy crisis is very symbolic. I think it's one of the ways in which nature is trying to say, 'Look, your souls are used up.' I think we're heading into a period where spiritually the lights are out."

"But don't you think God can still save us? I mean, isn't God the ultimate hero?"

Daniel Berrigan laughed. "God the ultimate hero?

Man, I don't know where you get your ideas. If he's anything, God is the ultimate servant."

We went downstairs. I had a drink before dinner. Berrigan had a drink before dinner. I had another drink before dinner. Berrigan had another drink before dinner. I had another drink before dinner. I am not sure whether Berrigan had another drink before dinner. Then there was wine with the meal. A lot of wine. To go with the thick roast beef. Normally, Berrigan said, he was a vegetarian. But tonight he was making an exception. I poured more wine. Berrigan was talking about how, when he had got out of prison, one of the things that struck him most forcefully was how most American faces out on the street—the kinds of faces he had not seen for two years—looked the same. How they had no character, no definition, no interest. "They were like this," he said, pointing to his plate. "Just big slabs of beef on top of collars."

He looked at me across the table. "Now you," he said, "have an interesting face."

I nodded.

"But I wonder," he said. "I wonder what it will look like in ten years."

After dinner we had after-dinner drinks. Then we left the dining room and walked across the hotel lobby to the bar. I ordered beer. Berrigan was drinking scotch. We were talking fast and laughing a lot. We ordered another beer, another scotch.

I had begun to notice, as I proceeded with my search, that it was not only I, the searcher, who seemed to enjoy a drink or two from time to time. I recalled my flight back to Washington with George

McGovern. And his remark in the motel room about drinking vodka and tonic during his campaign. And I recalled my lunch with Eugene McCarthy. And sitting up all night with William Styron. And here, now, was Daniel Berrigan staying just about even with me, glass for glass. I wondered: did they drink, as I often did, in order to shore up belief in their illusions? Was illusionless reality—life without myth—the same dark, empty, pit for them—the novelist, the priest, the candidates for President—that it was for me? I had another beer. Berrigan had another scotch. He was warm, funny, a real Irish storyteller. And not at all self-righteous, as I had feared. We stayed in the bar until two o'clock in the morning when they closed it. Talking about everything: God and children and sex and death and prison and Nixon and Jesuits and poetry and Nancy and wine and mountains and Vietnam. And, sweet Jesus, *we understood it all.*

The next morning, to get things back in focus, I opened the notebook into which I had transcribed the conversational highlights of the night. But, ho!—it was not my notebook at all. Apparently, someone had snuck into my room while I slumbered and had spirited *my* notebook away, leaving in its place a notebook which appeared, at first glance, to be identical—same size, same blue cover, same spiral binding—but which contained not the disciplined, accurate notes of a trained professional, but, rather, the tortured, illegible scribblings of someone who obviously had entered the terminal stages of Parkinson's disease. From what apparently had been the third predinner martini all the way to the immensely fraternal 2:00-a.m. departure scene, the notes might as well have been written in Chinese. It appeared, in fact, that significant portions of them had been written in Chinese. Thus, page after page of Daniel Berrigan's most telling insights, most profound speculations upon the nature of man and the universe, most self-revealing confessions, most memorable examples of wit, warmth, and humanity—lost to posterity. Oh well, like my headache, it was just another part of the price one paid for quick intimacy.

Then, as I closed the notebook to put it away, I noticed one exception: clearly printed in large, block letters and enclosed in three of four boldly drawn boxes, which apparently had been designed to call attention to it as a remark of extreme significance, was the phrase: MOOSESHIT, BUT GOOD.

I went home. Mooseshit, but good. It did not seem much to take with me. As I was getting on the plane to Toronto, I remembered that it had been the punch line to a joke. Daniel Berrigan had told the joke in the bar at the hotel after dinner. I had laughed loudly and for a long time. But now, even though I tried all the way to Toronto, I was not able to remember the joke. Also, I was not able to imagine what my face might look like in ten years.

The phone rings. Three nights before Christmas, 1971. Nancy and I have just decorated our Christmas tree. It is a small tree, and slightly tilted, and there are no presents underneath it, but the lights are nice. I answer the phone. It is my wife. She is calling from the Bryn Mawr Hospital in Bryn Mawr, Pennsylvania, twenty minutes from Swarthmore in light traffic. She has just brought Suzi, our three-year-old daughter, to the hospital. Suzi has a nosebleed that will not stop. She is pale and weak. And she has little red and purple spots beneath her skin. My wife is saying something about platelets. She is a nurse. She understands about platelets. They are elements in the blood which enable it to clot. You are supposed to have hundreds of thousands of platelets in every cubic millimeter of your blood. It has been determined at Bryn Mawr Hospital that Suzi, my three-year-old daughter, has almost none. . . .

I drove to Swarthmore. To my other life, my other self. I went to the hospital every day. I slept in my old house every night. My mother was there. A Christmas visit. Suzi's disease was called idiopathic thrombocytopedic purpura. Or, for convenience' sake, ITP. A virus was chewing up her platelets. When the virus went away she would get better. Meanwhile, her nose bled all the time. The doctors had to cauterize a blood vessel to make it stop. She was getting transfusions. And cortisone. And many many blood tests. She had large purple bruises where needles had been stuck into her arms and legs. They were sticking needles into her all the time. They talked about removing her spleen. I read to her and drew pictures with her and played games with her. Every day. She remained pale and weak and continued to bleed beneath her skin. She was brave. She was lonely. She was three years old and she was scared. Some nights she would cry as I was leaving. Some nights she would not.

I stayed in Swarthmore for ten days. I sat at my old place at the dining-room table. My older daughter, who was five, remembered when I had used to sit there every night. My son, who was fourteen months old, did not remember. I had gone away seven months before he was born. One day, my wife put some shirts of mine into the laundry. Shirts that Nancy had been taking out to have cleaned. Nancy's last name was on the collar of each as a laundry mark. When the shirts were dry, my wife crossed this out with heavy black ink.

I go to the hospital New Year's morning. The day is windy, cold, and clear. Suzi is cheerful. She holds a tissue to her nose. She seems always to be holding a tissue to her nose. Since the nosebleeds, tissues have become her security blanket. She tells me she dreamed of angels the night before. The angels had been singing "Silent Night." This renews my fear that she will die.

The blood specialist arrives. He is a tall, gentle man and Suzi is immensely fond of him. There is, however, an unpleasant task to be performed. The persistence of certain symptoms, and Suzi's failure to respond to medication, have forced the specialist to admit the possibility that she might have something worse than ITP. He must extract a sample of bone marrow to find out.

"It's going to hurt," he tells her softly, holding out a hand for her to grasp.

"I know. My daddy told me."

"But it's not like your regular blood test. It's not something we're going to keep doing every day. It's something we only have to do once."

She nods, her eyes wide. Trusting. Suzi has large, lustrous, brown eyes. When she first learned to talk, my wife and I would say to her: "Suzi? What are those eyes going to do to them?" And she would reply: "Knock 'em dead." She has had many needles stuck into her since she has been in the hospital, but this will be the first one stuck into a bone.

Two nurses came in and place her, face down, on a table. Then they roll the table down the hall, into a room with a larger table. Then they put her on the larger table. I am with her, holding her hand. One of the nurses swabs her hip with alcohol. The blood specialist takes a needle from a bag. It is the longest needle I have ever seen. It is the needle that will go into her hip bone to suck out the marrow. I am looking at Suzi now and making sure that Suzi is looking at me. I do not want her to see the needle. The blood specialist does not want her to see it, either.

Now he is ready. The two nurses grip Suzi firmly from either side. She must be held still while the marrow is extracted. I squeeze her hand lightly and pat her head. Then the doctor forces the needle into her bone.

When it is over and she is back in her room and her screaming has stopped, and he has gotten the marrow to the laboratory, the blood specialist comes in to see her. He tells her he is sorry it hurt so much. She pulls him toward her and hugs him and kisses him. And as he is leaving she says softly, from behind her security tissue: "Happy New Year." Two hours later he tells me the marrow sample is fine and I leave and drive back to Nancy.

A week after I saw Daniel Berrigan, I went to Columbia, South Carolina, to visit William Westmoreland. I went to his office, which was in a building owned by a bank. Westmoreland was serving as chairman of the Governor's Task Force on Economic Growth, and waiting to be asked to run for governor himself. He was expecting me. He stood as I entered the room. He was still trim at fifty-nine, his posture still flawless. His dominant features seemed unchanged: the jutting chin, the brow that overhung his dark, hard eyes like a shield. But about the face, where there had been only sharp bone and taut skin, there now was a suggestion of flesh. His hair, silver-colored, combed straight back, was longer than I'd expected. Then I realized that until now I never had seen him without a hat. I had, in fact, never seen him out of uniform, and there remained so much of the military in his bearing that to find him this way, in plain gray suit and dull necktie, was somehow disconcerting.

87

"Hi, general. Nice to see you again."

He did not smile as we shook hands. His gaze was hard, his mouth a thin straight line. He motioned to a table across the room. We took seats on opposite sides, and he waited for me to begin.

"I guess you know I'm going to be around for a few days."

"Yes. You were in Vietnam, weren't you?"

"A couple of times. I spent a day with you there in 1967."

"I remember. You wrote an article about me. In fact, I think it was two or three articles."

"No, just one, but it was long."

"Yes. Some friends of mine sent me copies." His eyes had not flickered. His words were toneless and flat. He said: "I remember that article." I nodded. I remembered it, too.

SAIGON, DECEMBER 1967—The black car moved smoothly across the concrete airstrip and stopped in front of the building. A United States Army captain, whose hair was cut so short you could not see it, climbed quickly out of the front seat, walked to the left rear door and opened it, and held a brown leather briefcase out before him. William Westmoreland, the commander-in-chief of the United States ground troops in Vietnam, got out of the car. The captain handed him the briefcase, and he walked, with long, certain strides, toward the front door of the building. When he got to the door, he stopped and looked at his watch. It was 1:45 in the afternoon. "I've got fifteen minutes," William Westmoreland said. "I'm going inside to do some work." The captain stepped in front of him and opened the door and William Westmoreland disappeared inside the building.

"He seems preoccupied today," a man standing on the airstrip said. "Well, you never know. Some days, he's loose as a goose."

At 1:58, a two-engined turboprop with four silver stars on its side taxied to a stop on the airstrip. Exactly two minutes later William Westmoreland came out the door he had gone in. He handed his briefcase to the captain and walked up the three steps that led from the airstrip to the plane.

The plane, a C-21, was built to hold six passengers, three in regular seats on the right side and three on a canvas bench across the aisle. William Westmoreland sat in the middle seat on the right side. The captain handed him a copy of Stars and Stripes, the armed forces newspaper, and a pair of earplugs in a small plastic bottle. Westmoreland held the plugs in one hand and looked at the headline of the paper.

"CHAPMAN USMC HEAD," said the heavy black letters across the top of the front page. For the first time since he arrived at the airstrip, William Westmoreland smiled.

"Good," he said. "I'm glad they got that settled. That dispute was threatening to wreck the Corps."

Then he looked across the aisle of the plane. "Do you know?" he said incredulously, "they were accusing me of plotting to pick a man for that job?"

He paused, staring, awaiting a response.

"As if you had nothing else to do."

William Westmoreland laughed. It was a happy,

honest laugh. "As if I had nothing else to do," he said. He laughed again. Then he went back to his paper.

The plane raced its engines and charged noisily down the runway which was baking listlessly in the Saigon sun. With one thrust it was in the air, then banked sharply to the left so that the muddy rivers that curled to the south of Saigon seemed to rise, steadily, like the upper half of a hospital bed, from the horizon. The plane straightened and moved, at a hundred and eighty miles an hour, to the east.

William Westmoreland turned the pages of the paper quickly, reading beyond the headlines only when he got to the sports. After ten minutes, he folded the paper and put it on his lap.

"How long have you been over here?" he said.

"Almost a month."

"Almost a month? Oh, well, you should be a real expert by now."

He paused, waiting for the laugh. When it came, he supported it with one of his own.

"Actually," he was told, "I know a lot less now than I did before I got here. About the only absolute I have left is that there are no absolutes."

"That's true," William Westmoreland said. "That's very true. You just can't generalize about this. Why, you can find facts to support any point of view you want to take."

"And people do."

He laughed again, over the noise of the plane. "And people do. Yes, they certainly do."

Then William Westmoreland opened the plastic bottle and put the plugs in his ears.

Half an hour later, the plane landed at Phan Thiet, on the east coast of Vietnam. Turquoise water could be seen breaking white against the shore.

"The first brigade of the 101st Airborne is out here," William Westmoreland said. "Just moved in a week ago. Route One runs right past here and we're trying to keep the VC away so we can open it to commercial traffic. General Matheson, who you see waiting for me out there, is in charge. He served in my brigade in Korea." Then William Westmoreland stood and the captain handed him a belt which held a pearl-handled knife and a pistol, and he put the belt around his waist and stepped off the plane.

"The last time General Matheson and I were together," he said, as the jeep rolled dustily toward brigade headquarters, "was two weeks ago, in the White House. We were both guests there for a weekend."

The jeep stopped and William Westmoreland got out.

"Where's my briefcase?" he said to the captain.

"I left it on the plane, sir."

"Why, dad-gum it, I'm going to need that briefcase."

"I'll get it, sir. Right away."

"Yes, we can send the jeep right back," General Matheson, a red-faced, pleasant man, said.

"I think you'd better," William Westmoreland said. "I'm going to need that briefcase."

"Yes, sir," the captain said, and hopped back in the jeep and left, raising dust behind him.

Ten minutes later, William Westmoreland was sitting on a chair in the front row of a briefing tent, eating a chocolate-chip cookie and drinking tea from a paper cup and looking at a big map, which said, at the top, "Operation Klamath Falls."

First one colonel, then another, then a captain, then a major, then another major, with occasional assistance from General Matheson, who was sitting on William Westmoreland's right, explained how the different parts of Operation Klamath Falls were working.

"Now, this next phase, sir, which was originated by our planning board—"

"It was originated by me, major," William Westmoreland said, "but go ahead."

Laughter filled the tent.

Then a Special Forces colonel named Griffiths, who had a long, deep scar on the right side of his scalp, got up to talk. He happened to mention something about the South Vietnamese Army—the ARVN.

William Westmoreland leaned forward in his chair. "Yes," he said. "The ARVN. How would you say they're performing?"

"Well, they're improving, sir," Colonel Griffiths said.

"They're improving. Uh-huh." William Westmoreland looked across the aisle of the tent at his guest. "They're improving," he repeated. "Well, would you say they're performing well?"

Colonel Griffiths looked at the floor of the tent. He opened his mouth and closed it and opened it again and took a deep breath and finally he looked up and answered. "No, sir," he said. "I couldn't say they're performing well."

William Westmoreland flicked away the reply,

like a championship boxer dismissing a sparring partner's jab.

"But they are improving," he said.

"Well, yes, sir," Colonel Griffiths said unhappily. "I mean, sir, when we get to a new location now, they're more likely to dig in before they put up their hammocks."

There were smiles in the tent but no one laughed. William Westmoreland was not among the smilers.

"How are they under fire, colonel?"

"Oh . . . better sir." Griffiths was getting desperate now, but with the coolness that Special Forces officers have when they are in trouble, he recalled an incident that could save him.

"Last week, sir, one of their lieutenants was shot in the leg. Pretty badly wounded, sir, and he refused evacuation for four days so he could stay with his men."

William Westmoreland turned quickly toward Colonel Griffiths.

"You say he refused evacuation for four days?"

"Yes, sir," Griffiths said.

"Well, that's wonderful. That's outstanding." William Westmoreland again looked across the aisle at his guest. "But that kind of story," he said, "never gets in the papers back home."

Now he swung sideways in his chair and began to make a speech to everyone in the tent.

"I was back in the States just two weeks ago, and let me tell you, what I read there, and heard there about the ARVN was horrifying. It was a horrifying and distorted picture. And that's because this kind of story, the story of performance like this, never gets printed in the papers."

He turned back to Colonel Griffiths. "Tell me, Colonel, did you relate this incident to any responsible reporter from a newspaper?"

Poor Griffiths. He had thought he was out of the woods. "Well . . . ah, yes, sir, to an Army reporter."

"To an Army reporter. But that's all? Not to any civilian reporter?"

"No, sir. I never had contact with any."

William Westmoreland looked back at the map in front of the tent. "Well, it's just a shame that this kind of story never gets in print. You can bet that if that lieutenant had turned around and run when the fighting started there would have been plenty of civilian reporters around."

There was silence in the tent. It hung heavily for a long time. Finally, General Matheson nodded, and another colonel began to speak, about Operation Niagara, which would follow Operation Klamath Falls.

When the briefing was over, Westmoreland decided that instead of going back to Saigon right away he would visit a battalion in the field. The ride was twenty minutes by helicopter, away from the coast, into the bushy green mountains that rose suddenly from the paler green plain.

The battalion's command post was marked by an American flag that rose high above the radio tent and waved in the afternoon breeze. William Westmoreland got out of the helicopter and strode quickly up a grassy hill to the battalion's briefing tent. Hot, dirty GIs trotted toward him with cameras, taking pictures as fast as they could. He listened to the briefing for ten minutes, then called to the battalion commander:

"Colonel, is that your idea? To fly the flag up there?"

"Yes, sir," the colonel said proudly.

"Well, I don't think it's a very good idea," William Westmoreland said. "If I were a VC mortarman sitting up in those hills that flag would make a damned good target for me, wouldn't it?"

"Yes, sir," the colonel said more softly.

"I might not be able to spot your radio antenna but I sure as hell could see that flag."

"We'll take it down, sir."

And, two minutes later, when William Westmoreland stepped out of the briefing tent and continued up the hill, the flag was down.

He stopped at the radio tent, which had a wall of sandbags four feet high around it.

"No overhead cover here?" William Westmoreland said.

"Sir, we're traveling kind of light and didn't bring overhead cover with us."

"And you can't get any locally?" He gestured toward the tree line about a hundred feet away.

"Well, it would take quite a bit of effort, sir."

"This is your radio tent. I think it's worth the effort to provide maximum possible protection here. I don't like to hear that men are afraid to sweat. You are good troopers. You fought damned well in I Corps. You did a job to be proud of there. But I hate to see good men slipping because they're lazy. I think you should have overhead cover for your radio tent."

"Yes, sir."

William Westmoreland moved on to inspect the five artillery batteries in the camp. The rest of the *battalion was out on patrol. In the third battery, the third man in line had no dogtags.*

"Where are your dogtags, son?"

"In my tent, sir."

"What are they doing there?"

"Well, sir, we're doing a lot of bending out here, and they seemed to get in the way, sir."

"Seemed to get in the way, huh?"

"Yes, sir."

He moved to the next man in line and reached beneath his shirt.

"Where are your dogtags?"

"In my tent, sir."

"Why?"

"Same reason, sir."

William Westmoreland stepped back one step and looked at the battery and at the sergeant in charge.

"I don't think that's a very good reason. I don't think that's a good reason at all. Dogtags are supposed to be worn at all times. Aren't they, sergeant?"

"Yes, sir."

"And they will be from now on, won't they, sergeant?"

"Yes, sir."

To the men in line: "Won't they?"

"Yes, sir," they said, sweatily, together.

"I don't like to see laxity out here," William Westmoreland said, and moved on to the fourth battery. On the way, a bareheaded private crossed his path.

"Where's your helmet, soldier?"

The private, who had curly brown hair, stopped. "In my tent, sir."

"What's it doing there?"

"I didn't think I needed it just to walk across here, sir."

"Helmets," William Westmoreland said, *"are to be worn at all times in the field. Where's your weapon?"*

"Back there, sir."

William Westmoreland stepped away from the private. *"Colonel,"* he called, *"this man is walking around without either his helmet or his weapon. This is exactly the kind of laxity I do not want to see. This does not come up to the standards of discipline that I want to see maintained by my men. This is totally unsatisfactory."*

"Yes, sir," the colonel said.

"It does not measure up to my standards at all."

"Yes, sir."

William Westmoreland spun, and continued on his way. . . .

"Of course," Westmoreland said. "That was a long time ago."

Yes, I agreed, it was. And far away.

Three days later, Nancy and I were riding in a car with William Westmoreland. We were riding in the back seat. Westmoreland was riding in the front. He was on his way to make a speech. His aide, a retired colonel, was the driver. It was the Tuesday before Thanksgiving. Nancy had come down the night before to take pictures to go with a magazine story I was planning to write about Westmoreland. Suddenly, he turned and asked if we had any special plans for Thanksgiving.

"No, general. Nothing special."

Then he began to talk about his new mountain cabin in North Carolina. About how pretty it was up there at this time of year. About the lake, and the big mountain behind the lake, and the woods, and the tennis, and the golf.

He said: "Normally, of course, our children are with us for Thanksgiving, but this year it just hasn't worked out that way, and I was wondering—and I'm sure Mrs. Westmoreland would be delighted— maybe, if you two really didn't have any special plans . . . It really is rather pleasant up there. I'm quite certain you would find it appealing."

I looked at Nancy.

Nancy looked at me.

I said: "Why sure, General. We'd love to."

So Wednesday afternoon we were driving a rented car along a lonely, hilly, two-lane blacktop road in North Carolina. Ahead of us, William Westmoreland was driving his new blue Audi, loaded with food for the weekend. Mrs. Westmoreland was by his side. We were driving to the mountains for Thanksgiving. Westy and Kitsi and Nancy and Joe.

The Audi slowed, then came gradually to a stop on the shoulder at the right side of the road. Westmoreland unfastened his shoulder harness, opened the door, climbed out, and walked slowly toward us, looking grim.

"What's up?" Nancy asked.

"I don't know. Maybe he's changed his mind."

I rolled down my window. It had rained hard earlier in the day, but now the sky had cleared. The afternoon was windy and very cool. William West-moreland approached.

"We've encountered a slight difficulty," he said, grinning.

"Oh?"

"We appear to have run out of gas."

The one-gallon can I brought back from the gasoline station we had passed ten minutes earlier had a short nozzle. The new blue Audi had a recessed tank. There appeared to be no way to transfer the gasoline from the can to the tank. I stood, holding the can, staring at the Audi's gas tank. William Westmoreland, of whom it had been admitted even by his critics that throughout his military career he had displayed a certain icy compe-tence when it had come to logistics, stood next to me, rubbing his chin with one hand, and stared at the gas tank, too.

"Oh boy," I said.

"Doggone," Westmoreland said.

"What do we do now?"

Westmoreland considered the available options for a moment. "I'm afraid," he said, "that you'll have to drive back there and try to get a different can. Or see if you can't borrow a funnel."

"Okay."

"I don't know what else we can do."

"Right."

Just then Nancy got out of our car. "For heaven's sake," she said. "You're standing practically in the middle of a garbage dump. Just get a beer bottle and break off the bottom and use that as a funnel."

"Hey!" I said.

"Good idea!" said William Westmoreland.

I found a bottle and handed it to him. Crouching, he cracked it against a rock. The bottom shattered. We had a makeshift funnel with jagged edges. Westmoreland inserted the neck of the bottle into the mouth of the gas tank. I placed the mouth of the gasoline can against the jagged open bottom of the bottle.

"Okay," Westmoreland said, "start to pour."

I tipped the can up and gasoline began to flow slowly through the bottle and into the tank.

"A little faster," Westmoreland said.

I poured faster. Gasoline flowed more rapidly into the tank. Too rapidly. The funnel overflowed and gasoline splashed out of it, onto Westmoreland's hands, my hands, and onto Westmoreland's highly polished shoes and the cuffs of his crisply pressed suit.

"That's all right," he said, grinning. "Full steam ahead." Then he looked at Nancy and me and he laughed, as gasoline continued to splash on the ground all around us.

It was dark by the time we reached the Blue Ridge Mountains and the condominium area within which the Westmoreland's cabin was located. A security guard at the entrance greeted Westmoreland, then waved us through behind him. We parked at the cabin, at the base of a mountain near a lake. Nancy and I helped the Westmorelands unload their car. Then Westmoreland went to a bedroom to change clothes. Then he borrowed firewood from a neighbor. Then he mixed us drinks. We took our drinks into the living room. He built a fire. We sat by the television set and drank our drinks and watched the news. First one network, then another.

A banner hung from a living-room rafter in the cabin.

"Welcome Home Westy," the banner said.

"Where'd you get that thing?" the general asked Mrs. Westmoreland.

She looked at him oddly. "What do you mean, where did I get it?"

"That banner up there. The one that group in Charleston had made up for me. How did you wind up with it?"

"No group in Charleston made that banner."

"Sure they did. For when I got back from Vietnam."

"Your daughter and I made that banner for when you came home from Vietnam. We were holding it up at the airport when you stepped off the plane."

William Westmoreland stared again at the banner. "Isn't that funny," he said. "I always thought I got it from a group in Charleston."

Much later, with the fire down but still glowing, and Mrs. Westmoreland gone to bed, Westmoreland and Nancy and I sat around a coffee table, sipping drinks.

I said: "You certainly are well received in South Carolina."

"Yes, I think that's true."

"I guess it's kind of a welcome change after Washington. And the way things have been for you in the rest of the country."

"No, I think you'd be surprised. For example, I can't go into a commercial airport in this country without two or three people speaking to me. And only recently I was grand marshal of a parade up in Baltimore. It was a patriotic parade. They told me there were half a million spectators."

"Really?"

"Yes. Now two, three, or four years ago, if I had been grand marshal, you can be sure that all the antiwar elements would have been out there, doing their thing. But in this case there was not a single act of discourtesy. In fact, as I was recognized by the spectators, there was, in almost every case, simultaneous applause."

"That must have made you feel good."

"Yes. Of course, I don't think any of the animosity was ever personal. It was directed at me because of what I represented. That's not to say it was enjoyable, having those people waving placards, saying I was a killer of women and children, et cetera et cetera. But you can't let it get you upset. You just have to take it in stride."

I had drunk perhaps too many martinis, too much wine. I said: "I guess I've always wondered: What did you feel over there?"

"I beg your pardon?"

"What did you feel in Vietnam? As a human being. You know, not as a general, just as a person. What did you feel about all those people being killed?"

"I don't think I understand your question."

"I mean, being in charge over there, for four years, and knowing every day that what you really were in charge of was the killing of thousands of people. Did you *feel* anything while all of that was going on?"

He looked at me evenly. He did not seem offended.

"I didn't feel any guilt about it, if that's what you mean."

"I guess that's what I mean."

"No. I've never felt anything like that."

"I just wondered."

"Some people, I know, would say I should have. And maybe they're right. I don't know. But I never have felt any guilt. And I would attribute that to my forty years of military training. One of the purposes of that kind of training, quite frankly, is to eliminate the sort of feelings that you've described. And that, I happen to believe, is essential. Otherwise, we wouldn't have any soldiers."

"Do you miss it? I don't mean Vietnam. I mean the Army. Being a general, chief of staff, all that."

"I guess I miss it in a way," he said quietly. Then he looked up. "No," he said more firmly. "I don't let myself miss it. I've got to face life as it is today, and that's what I intend to do."

Not long afterward, we went to bed. I slid open a closet door, looking for a hanger for my pants. Inside, in a neat row, hung several pairs of William Westmoreland's Army fatigues: all crisply pressed and each shirt with four silver stars on the collar.

On Thanksgiving morning, we rode with the general to the condominium golf club. A day of hazy sunshine and very warm. Two men came out of a clubhouse and walked toward the golf course, pushing their golf bags across the parking lot in little carts. The general stopped his car and rolled down the window.

"Good morning. I'm General Westmoreland."

The two men said good morning.

"Looks like a beautiful day."

The two men agreed that it did.

"Going out to play, I see."

The men nodded.

"I'm coming back up in a few minutes. Going out to play myself." The general paused, apparently to allow the men to ask if he might care to join them. They remained silent.

"Yes, it's a beautiful day," the general repeated.

The men nodded.

"Well, I'll be back up in a few minutes. Maybe I'll catch up with you."

The men nodded a third time, and smiled at the general, and walked on toward the first tee.

It was almost time for Nancy and me to leave. I went into the living room, where William Westmoreland had some papers spread upon a table. He looked up.

"My memoirs," he said. "I'm going to get some work done on them the rest of the weekend."

I was holding a cup of coffee in my hand. There was bright sunlight shining through the window behind Westmoreland's back, causing me to squint.

"I'm almost finished," he said. "A few more months."

"Really?"

"Yes, and, incidentally, one thing I made sure to do at the start was to retain the movie rights."

"Movie rights?"

"Yes. I think quite a movie could be made from my experiences. Especially my experiences in Vietnam. Sit down," he said, gesturing toward a couch. "Sit down."

I sat. I still was squinting. I was holding the coffee cup on my lap. Westmoreland looked at me. He said: "Now I'm just throwing this out, you understand. I'm not looking for any commitment. But the way I would want to do it, I thought it might appeal to you. Because of your book about television and Nixon and image and all that."

"Yes?"

"You see, I think the movie should focus on the Vietnam portion of my career. And the point would be about the difference between the image and the reality of what went on over there. About how the people at home were so misinformed about the war, through the television coverage, and things like that, which gave a false image, while I, who had all the facts, couldn't get my message across. Does that make sense?"

"Yes, yes, that makes sense."

"I think the movie should be called: 'Vietnam— The TV War.' "

" 'The TV War'?"

"That's right. And I was wondering—now you understand this is just something I thought I'd throw out, and I'm not looking for a definite answer this morning either way, and as a matter of fact I've still got a lot more thinking to do about it myself—but do you think you might be interested in, possibly, writing the script?"

I took a long sip of coffee. I said: "I don't know, general. I've never written a movie script."

"That's all right." He laughed. "You can practice on me."

There was a pause. I took another sip of coffee. I said, "I don't know, general. I'm not sure the time is right for a movie about Vietnam in which you, ah, would be played by John Wayne."

"Oh, no, no," he said, laughing again. "Not John Wayne. I wasn't thinking of the John Wayne kind of thing at all."

Just then, Mrs. Westmoreland came into the living room from the kitchen. "Oh, no," she said, laughing, too. "Not John Wayne. I think it would have to be Paul Newman."

We left in early afternoon. It was a splendid day, seeming more like spring than late November. Mrs. Westmoreland packed lunch for us and we drove with the windows open, warm in the sun, through the hills for a hundred miles to the airport at Johnson City, Tennessee. We bought a six-pack of beer early in the trip and listened to country music all the way.

The morning I brought Suzi home from the hospital my wife said she wanted to talk to me upstairs. We went up and sat on Suzi's bed. Then she told me that my best friend had been killed in an automobile accident the night before.

It was January, but when I thought of Peter I thought of spring. I thought of the spring of 1960 when we were seniors in high school and all things seemed possible and Peter would borrow his father's MG on Saturday mornings and take the top off and we would go riding around Scarsdale in the sunshine, driving fast, the radio loud, wanting every girl we saw and thinking that someday soon—maybe tonight!—we would have them, and that then our happiness would be complete, because we already had everything else.

Then I thought of a spring in Washington, seven years later. Peter had come back from Vietnam and was out of the Army and was working in bars around Georgetown. He was in love again. He always found a new love in the spring. I had come down from Philadelphia to write a column and had stayed over. I had a six-month-old baby and ambition that was just starting to come alive. We went to a triple feature movie on Saturday morning: Laurel and Hardy, W. C. Fields, and the Beatles. We drank Beaujolais in our seats and laughed out loud: Peter, his new love, and I. Then we stepped out into the sunshine and wandered squinting through Georgetown on a Beaujolais high. I went into a record- and bookstore. I bought the new Beatles album and a collection of James Reston columns. The album was called *Sgt. Pepper's Lonely Hearts Club Band.* I had never listened to the Beatles much before. We went to Peter's new love's apartment and lay on the floor, a warm April breeze blowing above us. We drank more wine, ate some cheese, played the record. Occasionally, I would read aloud from James Reston. We were just drunk enough so that James Reston seemed profound. After a while, Peter and the girl went to her bedroom to make love. "A Little Help from My Friends" was playing loudly. I lay on the floor, full of wine.

Then I thought of the spring of 1970. That was my rich and famous spring. I had met Nancy only a few months before. We flew to Washington on a Friday night and Peter picked us up at the airport. We were tired from drinking all day and went to bed as soon as we got to his apartment. It was a basement apartment, and from inside it you could not even tell that it was spring. Peter woke us up at 3:00 a.m. He was with some girls. They were all drunk. They wanted us to join the party. Peter had a new love but things were not going smoothly and on this weekend he was not with her. These were other girls. Nancy and I got up and had a beer and played a record and Peter and I made a few phone calls to old friends. He did not seem to care about the girls. Soon, Nancy and I went back to bed.

I woke up when I heard a huge crash. It was seven o'clock in the morning. I went to the front room to find out about the crash. I saw Peter. He was standing in his underwear in front of the full-length mirror that had been leaning against the wall next to the phonograph. There were tears in his eyes. There was glass on the floor by his feet. He was very drunk. He stared at the shattered mirror, where his image had been before he had smashed it with his fists.

"Oh, shit," he said. "I wish I lived in Australia."

It was very cold the day he was buried. The cortege wound slowly toward the cemetery along scenic Westchester roads. Peter had not gone to Australia. He had gone to Connecticut instead, and had worked for the Republican candidate for governor. The Republican had been elected and had offered Peter a job. Peter had accepted. A bus had come down from Hartford, bringing people with whom Peter had worked. The governor had come in his limousine. Flags in Connecticut were flying at half-mast. Because of the governor, there was a police escort for the cortege. And in the little villages along the way, villages through which we had ridden

so often in Peter's father's MG, there were police-
men stationed at the intersections to hold up traffic
so the procession could pass.

"The poor guy," his mother said. "He was just at
the crest of his own little wave."

It was quick at the grave. Too quick. One minute
there were a hundred of us standing there, all around
him, and the next minute it was over and all of us
had to turn and walk away, up a hill. Leaving him
there with the workmen in the cold.

I went to Cambridge, Massachusetts, to see Tim Sullivan, who had been a prisoner of war. Five hundred and sixty-six prisoners of war had come home. Tim Sullivan was the only one who had enrolled at Harvard. He was taking graduate courses in sociology. He also was the only one who had gone to Holy Cross, where I had gone. He had been a class behind me there, and I had not known him. His plane had been shot down in November 1967. For the next five and a half years, while I was meeting Robert Kennedy and going to Vietnam and coming back and sitting in the hospital where Robert Kennedy died and quitting my newspaper job and writing a best-selling book and fathering children and meeting Nancy and leaving my wife and writing another book and making another trip to Vietnam and watching the last of my childhood illusions slip away, and beginning my search for the vanished American hero, Tim Sullivan had been locked up in a concrete cell in North Vietnam.

I went to his apartment. It was a small apartment in an old building on a back street in Cambridge. But he owned the building. He had bought it with some of his $75,000 back pay. He was still at a class when I arrived. His girl friend let me in. She was a stewardess for Eastern Airlines. He had met her three weeks after he had come back, while flying to Florida for a wedding. The apartment was messy. There were notebooks, textbooks, copies of *Playboy* and *Penthouse* on the floor. And sections of the previous Sunday's *New York Times.* There had been a front-page story in the *Times*: "P.O.W.'s a Year Later: Most Adapt Well." His girl friend gave me a beer. Then she started to wash a frying pan in the sink. "Oh, yeah," she said, "Tim has adapted real well. I think it's his nature. He doesn't get excited about too much."

When he got back from class we drove to Springfield, his home town. He drove a Mustang. All the prisoners of war had been given free cars for a year. The year was up. He could pay for the car if he wanted to keep it. He was not sure whether or not he would. His parents lived in a little house on Carew Street. Big dog, small yard. Lots of pictures of Tim, and of the other children, around the house. He had three brothers and one sister. All grown. His father had worked for the Post Office. He was retired. Tim Sullivan changed from sweater and jeans into a blazer and plaid pants. He was speaking that evening to a suburban Lions Club in East Longmeadow. He spoke to most of the groups that asked him. "It's no real strain," he said. "I guess I'll keep it up as long as people are interested. But I think it will come to a screeching halt when we get to summer."

He was big: six foot three, big bones, big hands. Very big hands. Had played basketball at Springfield Cathedral. Intramural football at Holy Cross. He had curly black hair, dark eyes. Tough man to box out under the boards. Nicknamed "Sully." Quiet, deliberate, well liked. "Solid, not shaky," a Holy Cross classmate said. Tim Sullivan said, "I volunteered for Vietnam just more or less for the hell of it. It was one of those opportunities that comes along. Why not go see what it's like?"

That night, the East Longmeadow Lions sang songs. They sang "Alouette." Then, in honor of Tim Sullivan, who was, the toastmaster said, "recently returned from an extended vacation overseas," they sang, "When Irish Eyes Are Smiling." Tim Sullivan told them he had forgotten to bring his speech. The East Longmeadow Lions did not mind. He talked for a while about those men still listed as missing in action and about how important it was not to forget them. Then he said he would be happy to answer questions. He talked slowly, in a low, nonemotive voice. Most of the time there was a slight smile on his face. He said it could have been worse, all in all. He said he was glad to be home. He said if the North Vietnamese had tortured him a lot he probably would have signed anything they had wanted him to sign. He did not talk about what he had done to occupy his mind during the nine months he was in solitary confinement. He said he had not been bothered by the peace movement. He said he always believed that someday he would be released. He said he didn't think he was having any problems of adjustment, but that he understood it was much tougher for the married men. He said the major change he had noticed since returning to the United States was that "There seems to be a lot more honesty floating around, especially among the young people. A lot more awareness." When he was finished, the East Longmeadow Lions gave him a standing ovation. Then they gave a standing ovation to the kitchen crew.

We drove back to Cambridge, past Worcester, where Holy Cross was located. Six weeks after his return from Vietnam, Tim Sullivan had spoken to an ROTC chapter at Holy Cross. He had been asked whether or not his four years at Holy Cross had in any way aided him during his captivity. He had thought for a moment, apparently about the extensive courses in Jesuit theology and philosophy which had been such a major part of the Holy Cross curriculum. Then he had said yes.

He had said: "After suffering through one kind of propaganda, the second time around is easy."

He had said: "Believe me, I had been through the same thing before."

Now, in the car, he said: "If you want to see hero worship, you ought to come back up when the Bruins win the Stanley Cup."

I had lunch with William Buckley at his town house in Manhattan. There was a touch of vodka before the meal, then an agreeable white wine. "Written any more bad novels lately?" Buckley asked. It happened to be a Holy Day of Obligation. Buckley said he trusted that I already had been to Mass. It was all very elegant in an understated way, except I had red all over my fingernails from having eaten too many pistachio nuts the night before.

Buckley said I should remain conscious of the distinction between hero worship and lionization. He said Whittaker Chambers certainly had seemed to be heroic. And that perhaps Solzhenitsyn was in our time. But he asked: "What are the reticulations by which you can locate the hero if you don't even know what the grid is?"

After lunch, he took me into his parlor and played a Goldberg Variation on his harpsichord. It was very pretty music. He played intently, and I sat in a chair off to one side. Outside, I could hear sirens and the honking of horns. When he finished, it was time for him to fly to the Midwest and make a speech. His chauffeur was ready with the car.

I went to Ohio to visit John Glenn, the first American to have orbited the earth. He lived in a nice new house by the river. Very modern. Lots of wood and glass. He was just starting to run again for the Senate. He was very friendly and he smiled a lot. He kept wanting to know who else I had seen and what they had said about heroes. "You saw Westmoreland? Yes? What did *he* say?" What had McCarthy said. And McGovern? He did not seem to be concerned with Daniel Berrigan.

He had been the greatest space hero we had known. The first. Ticker-tape parades, open cars with JFK. There had been high schools, freeways, children, household pets that bore his name. The John Glenn this and the John Glenn that. He had made the archetypal, mythic, heroic journey. To the secret realm of the gods and back again. Now he wanted to be a senator from Ohio. I wanted to know what illusions he had lost, or had found, on his adventure. I wanted to know what boons he had brought back. He told me I should be talking to James Reston.

He called Reston "Scotty." He said: "Heroes? You've really got to talk to Scotty on this." Then he went to his telephone and called Reston's private number. The person who answered was not Reston. "Can you tell me where I can reach him please? This is John Glenn." There was a pause. Then he grinned. "Yes," he said, "at least I *think* it's the same John Glenn." But Reston was not available.

We had dinner. Steak, potatoes, salad, garlic bread. White wine. John Glenn's wife was very nice. Everything was very friendly and relaxed. I learned that his favorite movie was *The Secret Life of Walter Mitty.* He talked about how America could be great again, and of how we could not afford to turn our backs on progress. He said ingenuity and perseverance were what counted. He said hero worship was fine as long as it was based not on illusion but on admiration for achievement. The whole thing was low key and, in a not unpleasant way, somehow Midwestern. I kept feeling that when dinner was over he would take me into the living room and try to sell me insurance.

But he was so genial, so concerned, that I stayed until one o'clock in the morning. He took me to his study and showed me lots of astronaut pictures and charts and things from his flight. He had the handle with which he had flown his space craft mounted as a trophy. He said: "This is the real one. The one in the Smithsonian is a fake."

He was patient, gracious, and quite sincere about wanting to help me. And I liked him, just as everyone had said I would. But the later it got, no matter how hard I tried to resist, the less he seemed like the first American to have orbited the earth and the more he seemed like the next junior senator from Ohio.

Then I went to Connecticut and sat up late with Arthur Miller. In Roxbury, where I had known him in 1970, during the one summer I had lived there. He talked about why there were no heroes any more. He said we had replaced God with technology, and now that technology had turned sour we were left with a sense of self-contempt. And there was no place for a hero in a world of self-contempt. Then he talked about why he still went out each day to the workroom that stands behind his house. About why, more than twenty-five years after *Death of a Salesman*, his play about the collapse of an illusion, and more than ten years after the death of Marilyn Monroe, the illusion he had married, he still labored to create.

He said: "Supposedly, you do it for your peers. But I have no peers any more. They're all gone. I do it because I have to do it. Because I can't bear living without it. The earlier impulses of proving yourself and of competing can only carry you so far. Then you realize that practically all of it is transient.

Written, produced, acted, and gone. If you keep going after that, I guess it's because you need to try to make something beautiful. To give form to the chaos of feeling that is your life.

"The problem is, you can never stop and say: 'There, I've got it.' The world is all new all the time. I go out there, and every day I'm starting all over again. I'm always an amateur. I start something, and then I realize I simply don't know how to do it. Every day I give up. But then I always come back to it again.

"Controlled hysteria is what's required. To exist constantly in a state of controlled hysteria. It's agony. But everyone has agony. The difference is that I try to take my agony home and teach it to sing."

The phone rings. Nancy and I are at Saratoga for the races. We have rented a house at the north end of town. Each afternoon we go to the racecourse and stand, sipping drinks, in the sun; and stroll across the grass, amid the elm trees, admiring the splendid young horses; and climb to our box seats in the old wooden clubhouse, from where we can see which of the horses is best. The phone rings at the rented house in early evening. It is my mother. She is frightened. Something is happening to my father.

He was forgetting things. He was having trouble reading. He had started to bump into things when he walked. Also, he had begun to speak strangely: in a monotone, and as though he were very far away. In the mornings, he would wake up and sit at the end of his bed, his head in his hands, staring at the floor and saying nothing. He would not answer my mother when she spoke. After a while he would stand up and put on a suit and go to his job in the city.

McGinniss Travel Service, of the Essex House, had gone bankrupt. It was no more. The gilt letters had been scraped off the window. My father had put all the money he had saved, and had inherited, into the business. He had mortgaged the house in Rye, cashed in his insurance policies, even sold his stamp collection. And it was gone. All of it. Except for a little bit of IBM. McGinniss Travel Service had become my father's private Vietnam. Now he was working at another travel agency, on commission, and earning almost no money at all. He did not even have any Blue Cross.

The first time I had told him I was leaving my wife, he cried. He, and my mother, had built this beautiful sand castle—made of my marriage, my children, my success. Then I had kicked it into pieces. Neither he nor my mother had recovered. They still went to Swarthmore to visit my children and my wife. They did not come to where I was to visit me. And now my father would not be visiting anyone, anywhere, ever again.

I talked to him the night my mother called.
"Mother says you haven't been feeling too well."
There was a long silence. Then he said: "That's . . . her . . . story." He spoke very slowly, with no inflection, as if he were reading aloud in a language he had just begun to learn.

Two days later he went into the hospital. I spoke to his new doctor, a neurologist. I explained that I was planning to write a book about Saratoga and that if I were forced to be away from the race meeting for very long I would have to cancel the contract. I said: "I guess what I'm trying to determine is how sick he really is. In other words, whether or not you think I should come home."

The doctor said: "I think it's time to come home."

So in mid-August heat I drove my mother to the hospital every day and we sat by my father's bed while he tried to read the papers and after a while we would walk down the corridor to a sitting room and sometimes go out onto a patio with my father in his bathrobe and slippers and me holding his arm to keep him walking straight. On the patio he would smoke and we would listen to the noise of the traffic on Boston Post Road. This was the hospital, in Port Chester, where he had been once before, years earlier, with rheumatic fever. The hospital in which I had had my tonsils and appendix removed. Across the Boston Post Road was the Korvette's where my father had gone each Saturday morning in the fall of 1969, when my first book was newly published, checking to see how many copies it had sold. Everyone had told me how proud of me he had been. We did not talk much on the patio. It did not seem as if there were much to say. After half an hour we would walk, very slowly, back to his room. His right slipper made a noise as it dragged along the corridor as we walked.

The doctor was extraordinary. He came in every day and talked cheerfully to my father and sympathetically to my mother, giving them strength without false hope, which was tricky. Then I would follow him into the corridor and he would tell me the truth: a brain tumor, apparently getting bigger in a hurry.

It was very hot. Outside the hospital the asphalt shimmered. I brought my mother home each night and cooked her dinner. Or else we would go to a restaurant. She was being much stronger than I had thought she would be. And she had no false hope. She knew what was going to happen. She was just getting stronger, that was all. I slept in the bed I had slept in as a boy, and slept poorly.

One day they shot dye into my father so they could see how big the tumor was and in what portion of his brain it was located. He spoke to us that evening from a distance that was greater than ever. He said the injection of the dye had hurt a lot.

The surgeon came in. He said he would operate in the morning. When he left, I helped my father down the corridor to the bathroom. He was much worse than he had been a week before. I had to almost carry him down the hall. Inside the bathroom I helped him off with his robe and guided him into a stall. When he was finished, I helped him up—he was heavy—and then, slowly, with great difficulty, I started him back toward his room. Halfway, we paused to rest. He leaned against a wall and I supported him. I realized I might not have another chance to speak to him alone. But I could not think of anything to say.

Finally, I told him that I loved him. He looked at me. Then he nodded. Then we continued our journey down the hall.

"Full circle," Joseph Campbell wrote in *The Hero*

with a Thousand Faces, "from the tomb of the womb to the womb of the tomb, we come: an ambiguous enigmatical incursion into a world of solid matter that is soon to melt from us, like the substance of a dream. And, looking back at what had promised to be our own unique, unpredictable, and dangerous adventure, all we find in the end is such a series of standard metamorphoses as men and women have undergone in every quarter of the world, in all recorded centuries, and under every odd disguise of civilization."

It was time to go. I stepped into the corridor so my mother could be alone with my father in the room. She did not stay long. When she came out she told me that as she was leaving he had started to cry. She had bent close to him and he had whispered: *"I'm . . . afraid."* I lay awake through most of that night, wondering if my father was awake, too. And wondering, from three miles away, what he was thinking.

He never was conscious again. Once, on the afternoon of the surgery, he opened his eyes and mumbled a few words which seemed to indicate that he thought that I was him when he had been my age. Then he went into a coma. It lasted for days. We would sit by his bedside for hours, watching him breathe, hearing him breathe, and nothing else. Some days he would be shaved. Some days he would not. Except for that, all days were the same. Nancy was at her parents' house in New Rochelle, not far away. Every so often I would drive down there. Once in a while we would go to a motel. Then I would go back to the hospital and sit and stare at my father. Occasionally, I'd squeeze his hand. Once or twice I thought I felt a faint squeeze in return. The doctor said this was a reflex: meant nothing.

The phone rang. At 6:45 on the morning of September 8. My mother's birthday. Nancy's birthday, too, as it happened. Miss Mulholland, the night nurse, was calling. She told me my father was dead. She asked if I would pick up his things.

When I got to the hospital, Miss Mulholland handed me a paper bag containing his slippers, bathrobe, shaving cream, razor, toothbrush, and some toothpaste which he had purchased at Korvette's. Then she asked if I wanted to see him before they moved him from the room. I said yes. I had seen him alive on several thousand mornings. On this one morning I supposed that I should see him dead.

He was pale. His eyes were closed. His mouth was open, as it had been for days, but his chest was not moving up and down. He was unshaven. He was dead.

His hands were on top of the sheets. I touched one. Then I went home. He had been dead for maybe an hour. After fifty-six years of being alive. His series of standard metamorphoses was over. His unique, unpredictable, and dangerous adventure was at an end. He had no more illusions to lose. I wondered again what he had thought about during that last night before the operation. I wondered again if he had slept. I wondered if he had wanted anyone to talk to.

I rode a bus to New York. It was a Sunday evening, warm for February, and light drizzle fell. I was going to see Joe R. Hooper, of Zillah, Washington, the most decorated soldier of the Vietnam war . . .

[CITATION, CONGRESSIONAL MEDAL OF HONOR]—*Company D was assaulting a heavily defended enemy position along a river bank when it encountered a withering hail of fire from rockets, machine guns and automatic weapons. Staff Sergeant Hooper rallied several men and stormed across the river, overrunning several bunkers on the opposite shore. Thus inspired, the rest of the company moved to the attack. With utter disregard for his own safety, he moved out under the intense fire again and pulled back the wounded, moving them to safety. During this act Staff Sergeant Hooper was seriously wounded, but he refused medical aid and returned to his men. With the relentless enemy fire disrupting* the attack, he singlehandedly stormed three enemy bunkers, destroying them with hand grenades and rifle fire, and shot two enemy soldiers who had attacked and wounded the chaplain. Leading his men forward in a sweep of the area, Staff Sergeant Hooper destroyed three buildings housing enemy riflemen. At this point, he was attacked by a North Vietnamese officer whom he fatally wounded with his bayonet. Finding his men under heavy fire from a house to the front, he proceeded alone to the building, killing its occupants with rifle fire and grenades. By now his initial body wound had been compounded by grenade fragments, yet despite the multiple wounds and loss of blood, he continued to lead his men against the intense enemy fire. As his squad reached the final line of enemy resistance, it received devastating fire from four bunkers in line on its left flank. Staff Sergeant Hooper gathered several hand grenades and raced down a small trench which ran the length of the bunker line, tossing grenades into each bunker as he passed by, killing all but two of the occupants. With these positions destroyed, he concentrated on the last bunkers facing his men, destroying the first with an incendiary grenade and neutralizing two more by rifle fire. He then raced across an open field, still under enemy fire, to rescue a wounded man who was trapped in a trench. Upon reaching the man he was faced by an armed enemy soldier whom he killed with a pistol. Moving his comrade to safety and returning to his men, he neutralized the final pocket of enemy resistance by fatally wounding three North Vietnamese officers with rifle fire. Staff Sergeant Hooper then established a final line and *reorganized his men, not accepting treatment until this was accomplished and not consenting to evacuation until the following morning. . . .*

He was staying at the McAlpin Hotel, which was a big old hotel, near Penn Station, and not classy. Joe Hooper was staying there with his wife and with a little dog that belonged to his wife. He had just got out of the Army. He was thirty-four years old and he was on his way home to Zillah. In high school, at Moses Lake, he had set a state record for most touchdowns scored in one season. For a while, he had held the national high-school record for the one-mile run. He was six feet tall, he had blond hair and blue eyes. He had killed approximately 115 men in Vietnam. Some, he had killed with a bazooka, some with grenades, some with a rifle, some with a knife. One, he had thrown from a helicopter "because he laughed at me." He had killed twenty-four men in a single afternoon. For that, to go with his seven Purple Hearts, three Vietnamese Crosses for Gallantry, two Silver Stars, one Bronze Star, one Vietnamese Presidential Citation, and one Army commendation medal, he had been awarded his Congressional Medal of Honor.

I met him in the hotel lobby. His wife was with him. There was very little carpeting in the lobby and what there was was worn. He had been discharged a week earlier from Fort Polk, Louisiana, and had driven to New York to see Joe Frazier fight. Frazier had been heavyweight champion at one time. He and Joe Hooper had been among the subjects of a magazine article that dealt with the minds of men who were paid to be violent. Frazier had sent Joe Hooper tickets to the fight. Joe Hooper's wife had bright red hair and pale skin and she stooped forward as she walked. She was from Alabama, and once had worked for George Wallace. She had a disease of the spine called ankylosis spondylitis. A doctor at Fort Polk had told her it was incurable. That she would get more and more stooped and be in more and more pain all the time and that in three years she would be dead.

We went to the Press Box, a steak restaurant on the east side. Joe Hooper walked with a check for $12,000 in his shoe. It was his Army retirement pay. He had been given the check at Fort Polk and had not been able to get it cashed in New York. I ordered a martini before dinner and he ordered a double gin and tonic. He drank it very fast and ordered another. Then a third.

"Honey, tell him about when Nixon gave you the medal."

"Oh, yeah." Joe Hooper laughed. He laughed loudly and his head moved and rocked back and forth as he laughed. This was after dinner. We were friends by this time and laughing a lot. There had been wine and beer and Irish coffee and now Joe Hooper was drinking gin and tonics again—"Make mine a double, no, a triple"—and so was I.

"I come in there for the ceremony, you know, and I'm smashed. I been up all night. Hell, I don't think I slept in two days. So Nixon comes over to chat a little before the official thing starts—there was me and two other guys, I think, getting the medals—and it's only eleven o'clock in the morning, you know, and my breath—damn—it nearly knocks him over.

So he starts looking at me funny and I'm thinking, Oh shit—because I always heard he was kind of stiff and proper, you know?—but he just smiles and says, 'I don't know what you've been drinking there, sergeant, but it sure smells good.' So I say I got plenty more in my flask. And he says yeah? And I say sure thing, you want a drink? And he says yeah. So we go into this little room off the main room there and he shuts the door. And I take out the flask and he takes a belt and so do I. Then we go back out and he gives me the medal. I'll tell you, pardner—ever since then I always figured Nixon was okay."

Time passed. "Listen," I said, "I've got to go. I've got to catch a bus."

"You can't go. You haven't even interviewed me yet."

"I'll call you in a day or two. We can get together. But this is the last bus."

"The night hasn't hardly started."

"Nancy's expecting me."

"Call her. Tell her you're gonna interview Joe Hooper the Medal of Honor winner, the most decorated soldier of the Vietnam war."

"She already knows that. I'm supposed to be finished by now."

"Well it ain't my fault if all you do is talk and drink and eat instead of interviewin'."

"I've got to catch the bus."

"You can stay with us. Sleep on the floor in our room. Ain't that right, baby?"

"Why of course, Joe, if he wants to. But maybe he really does have to catch the bus."

"He don't have to catch the bus. All he's got to do is make a phone call."

"I really should catch the bus."

"Here I am tryin' to cooperate and give you an exclusive interview and you're runnin' out on me. I don't think that's very polite."

"Now, Joe, let him go if he wants to."

"It's not that I want to. But I've got my car parked at the bus stop and Nancy needs it in the morning, and—"

"All . . . you got to do . . . is go over . . . to the damn telephone . . . and call up, and say you're with Joe Hooper, and you're not gonna be able to catch the bus."

"If you keep arguing with him, Joe, he'll miss it anyway."

"Hey, that's right. Wow. I've only got about twelve minutes."

"That settles it. You never would have made it anyway. Go call. You have any trouble, I'll talk to her. Then you come right back here pardner and we'll get ourselves a couple drinks."

I called. Then I went back to the table. Joe Hooper said, "I'll tell you who my hero is: Art Buchwald."

"Art Buchwald!"

"I think the man's a damn genius."

"Art Buchwald is your hero?"

"Honey, remember that one article he wrote about the war? The one where he explained how screwed up everything was?"

"Which one was that, Joe?"

"You know the one I mean. The one I tore out and carried around in my wallet. Damn. I never thought I'd laugh so hard."

"This is amazing."

"A damn genius. He sees right through everything, that guy. I tell you, that's one man I'd really like to meet someday. Say, where's he live? Washington?"

"This is amazing. Listen, Nancy's coming into the city tomorrow. The reason she's coming in is because she's writing a story for a newspaper in Philadelphia about Art Buchwald."

"You're shittin' me."

"He's taping a David Susskind show tomorrow afternoon. Then he's going up to Hartford on a train. She's going with him."

"Is that right?"

"You really want to meet him?"

"You think I could?"

"Of course. We'll just go up to the Susskind studio and—hey! Here's even a better idea: is there anything you have to do tomorrow night?"

"We're supposed to see a couple of people. But it doesn't have to be tomorrow night."

"All right. Then here's what we'll do. We'll meet Nancy and Buchwald at the studio, and then we'll ride up to Hartford with them on the train. Bring a few drinks along, you know? Make it a party."

"Yeah?"

"It'll be great."

"Won't that mess up Nancy's interview?"

"No, no. It'll make it better. You know, much livelier."

"Do you know Art Buchwald?"

"Nope. Never met him."

"Then what makes you think he's going to want us to come along?"

"Are you kidding? He'll love it. He's a great guy. Everyone says so. He'll be thrilled."

"You really think so?"

"Of course. Don't forget: you're not just some stranger. You're Joe Hooper. The Medal of Honor winner. The most decorated soldier of the Vietnam war."

Time passed. It was five-thirty in the morning. Starting to get light outside. We were in Joe Hooper's hotel room. Drinking white wine. Warm and sweet. Joe Hooper's wife was in her nightgown. Her little dog barked at me. Joe Hooper and I had been out. His wife had been in bed, but because of the pain in her back she had not been able to sleep. Joe Hooper took off his shoes. He wanted to be sure he still had his check. The $12,000 check he could not cash. It was starting to get wrinkled and a little torn from being walked around on for so long.

"I spoke to the Boy Scouts down in Houston," Joe Hooper said. "I wish you could've seen it. They went wild. It's like that everywhere. When I go to a ball game or something. Dodger Stadium. They put it on the scoreboard that I'm there and, bang, that's the end of the ball game for me. Rest of the night all I'm doing is signing autographs. And like with jobs. I can write my own ticket. Practically anywhere. I got some offers you wouldn't believe. Three hundred thousand to go with some Italian firm. I forget the name. One of them big Italian firms. Then Hughes Aircraft. They want me to do p.r. Fifty-four thousand a year. Then there was a big insurance company. I turned them down. There was a hundred thousand a year to be like a factory representative for one of them aerospace companies, I better not mention the name. The thing is, everybody wants me. Everybody wants to say, look, this here is Joe

135

Hooper and we've got him. It gets to be kind of a burden, you know?"

"Yeah, yeah. I know."

"See then there's Hollywood. I could go to Hollywood and really make it. I project good on screen. They told me that. I met some big people in Hollywood. They said, 'You're a natural, come on in.' I already turned down a big offer. It was an anniwar film."

"A what? An Andy Warhol film?"

"An *anti war* film. I turned them down flat. Didn't want any part of it. Then I had an offer to get into politics. They wanted me to run for mayor."

"Who did?"

"These people."

"In Hollywood?"

"Beverly Hills. They still want me. They want me to be mayor of Beverly Hills."

Then he gave me a pen and a copy of his Medal of Honor design on one side and a facsimile Joe Hooper signature on the other.

Time passed. Four hours later, Joe Hooper was tucking his check into his shoe. Ready to start the new day. "Hey, pardner," he said. "How about a drink?" For the first time I noticed a pistol on a nightstand by the bed. Then I noticed a rifle leaning against a closet door. He explained that because of carrying such a large check around he thought he would be safer with a pistol. I didn't see what he was worried about. He couldn't even cash the check himself. I didn't see how anyone who stole it from his shoe would be able to. The rifle, he said, was a souvenir. He had taken it out to check the sight. He

136

checked the sight by pointing the rifle out his hotel-room window at the entrance to Gimbel's across the street. He stopped when he noticed that people at the entrance were beginning to stare.

"Hey, pardner, you sure we ought to do this with Art Buchwald?"

"Absolutely. It's a once-in-a-lifetime opportunity."

Time passed. We climbed down from our seats and walked quickly across the studio floor. Art Buchwald still was chatting with David Susskind. He was smiling and smoking a cigar. He glanced up and saw Joe Hooper, and me, and Joe Hooper's wife moving toward him. Joe Hooper and I had been drinking through most of the day. Art Buchwald stopped smiling when he saw us. I grinned and gave him a little wave. Nancy got to me just before we got to him.

"He doesn't want to do it."

"What do you mean he doesn't want to do it?"

"He's tired and he's got a big speech in the morning, and he just wants a quiet train ride and a good night's sleep."

"But that's ridiculous. He's Joe Hooper's hero."

I reached Buchwald's side. Joe Hooper and his wife were right behind me.

"Hi," I said, introducing myself. "Like you to meet a couple of friends of mine: Joe Hooper, and his wife, Faye Hooper. I guess Nancy told you, Joe is a Medal of Honor winner. In fact, he was the most decorated soldier of the whole Vietnam war."

"Yes, yes," Buchwald said. "How do you do."

"Joe's a great fan of yours. Really thinks you're

tops. I guess Nancy told you we were thinking of riding up to Hartford with you on the train. Maybe have a few drinks at the hotel when we get in."

"That wouldn't be such a good idea," Buchwald said. He puffed on his cigar. He seemed nervous. He was looking toward the studio doors.

"I mean, we wouldn't have to stay up all night or anything. It's just that Joe here—"

"Nancy, are you ready?" Buchwald said. "We've got to run." He shook hands with me quickly. "Been very nice meeting you . . . Mrs. Hooper, Mr. Hooper. . . ." Then he took another puff on his cigar and he was gone.

Time passed. I spent three more days and nights with Joe Hooper. His check became extremely wrinkled and somewhat stained. We went to a lot of places and we had a lot of drinks. The consumption of alcohol, in fact, had become the apparent purpose of our lives. We drank through the daytime and we drank through the night, and our illusions grew in wisdom and in strength.

Joe Hooper told stories. About how he had been flying home from Bolivia and had wanted his girl friend to meet him at the airport so he had sent her a telepathic message, giving his flight number and arrival time, and she had been there, waiting, when he arrived. And a story about a Saint Christopher's medal and a flame thrower and a miracle that saved dozens of lives. And a story about the spotlight he had seen whenever he had prayed during battle. And many more.

Time passed. It was three o'clock in the morning and we were in a bar where an old woman with a lined face was holding my hand and telling my fortune and Joe Hooper was telling me to shut up and pay attention because what the old woman was saying would come true. Then it was lunchtime and we were in a place that did not rush us, and we had many beers before lunch and then wine and Irish coffee and then brandy and then it was midafternoon, then late afternoon, and we were drinking beer again and we did not leave the restaurant until people began to come in for dinner. We went to Penn Station and bought tickets for the Washington train. I'm not sure why. But there we were in the parlor car, ordering drinks, and Joe Hooper was telling more stories and so was I and the train was speeding away, carrying us and our illusions into the night.

Sunday morning. I go to Mass with my wife. She is a nurse. She wears her white uniform to Mass. Afterward, I shall drive her to the hospital where she works. Every Sunday, I go to Mass with my wife. In the suburbs of Philadelphia. I live with her in a little apartment in the suburbs of Philadelphia. I ride a trolley to work in the mornings. There is a stop across the street from the apartment. I ride the trolley home at night. I work for a newspaper, writing about things that happen in Philadelphia, a city to which I do not belong. I sit and kneel and stand during Mass, like everyone else. I hear the priest talk. I have been hearing the priest talk all my life. I am twenty-four. It seems that I have gone directly from childhood to middle age. In the suburbs of Philadelphia. I feel I must go away soon and have adventures. . . .

AN LOC, SOUTH VIETNAM— *"I could have retired a year ago," Joe Stringfield was saying. "And I was* going to. Yessir, I had twenty years in and I was ready to go."

"What happened?"

"Well, I started thinking. You been in twenty years you hate to walk out in the middle of a war. Especially a war like this, where you don't know what the hell is going on. I couldn't figure it out. The papers, the TV, none of them made any sense. I guess that's really why I did it. I wanted to see what it was all about. So I figured I'd give it one more year and put in for over here. And I'm glad I did. Yessir, I'm glad I did."

It was Thanksgiving night, 1967. A clear night and the stars came early. I was lying in a tent with two sergeants. It was very dark inside the tent. Only two dots of orange from the cigarettes the sergeants were smoking could be seen. First one, then the other, would glow brightly for a moment, then fade, as the smoke was drawn through the tobacco and inhaled. The sergeants, Joe Stringfield and Joe B. Blackwell, were lying on their backs in the tent. Another sergeant stopped at the tent. Talk turned to the R & R center at Vung Tau, where Joe Stringfield and Joe B. Blackwell were planning to go together.

"How's the beach?" Joe Stringfield asked.

"Oh, real nice beach."

"And is there any bars around there, you know, with any broads in them?"

"Oh, yeah, right there. Place called The Beachcomber's the best one."

"The Beachcomber, huh?"

"Yup."

"What kind of broads? Vet-namese, or what?"

"Oh, all kinds. Vietnamese. French. Even some American broads."

"American broads? Really?"

"Yup, at least when I was there."

"How about that. What did you wind up with?"

"I got a little French chick. A schoolteacher."

"A French chick? Yeah?"

"Yeah, boy. She was all right."

"How the rooms where you stay?"

"Oh, real good. Two guys to a room and every one's got a bathroom with a shower."

"Hot shower or cold shower?"

"Cold shower."

"How about the chow?"

"Chow's real good."

"And is there any shows or stuff?"

"Yeah, when I was there they had a USO show from California. No broads in it, but some real good music."

"And you can pick this stuff up right in that Beachcomber?"

"Yeah, right there. Or right out on the beach. The beach is right across the street."

"Yeah?"

"Yup."

"Hey, Blackwell, this sounds pretty good. You still want to go there?"

"Okay."

Joe Stringfield lit another cigarette as the sergeant who had been to Vung Tau walked away. *"Yeah, that sounds all right,"* he said, and then it was quiet in the tent.

At four o'clock in the morning I would be going on

a patrol. I would be going with a hundred and thirty men from the battalion I was with. I would walk three miles through a rubber-tree plantation with these men in order to reach a particular village by dawn. There had been reports of Viet Cong in the village, and the colonel in command of the battalion wanted his men to surround the village and to shoot the Viet Cong as they tried to get away. The colonel had invited me to come along on the patrol and I had accepted. I had not told the colonel I was scared of the dark.

There was a whisper. A short, sucking whisper. It was fifteen minutes before midnight. The first whisper was followed immediately by another. "Mortar! Mortar!" The cry came from somewhere to the left. There was no chance to get to the bunker. Only to fall from the cot and to press against the sandbags that lined the outside of the tent.

"Sonofabitch!" Joe Stringfield said. Both he and Joe G. Blackwell were breathing hard and pressing as close as they could to the sandbags. Then everything was quiet.

"Hey," Joe B. Blackwell said after thirty seconds. "Those didn't go off."

"No," Joe Stringfield said, "They didn't."

"Think they were duds?"

"I don't know. Two duds in a row is kind of funny."

"Want to go down in the hole?"

"No. They seem to have stopped."

Then Joe Stringfield and Joe B. Blackwell crawled out from under their cots and brushed the dirt off their stomachs and lay down again, and this time there were three orange dots in the tent instead of two.

Another whisper—then a crash. WhisperCRASH! WhisperCRASH! These were not duds. Five rounds landed in the first five seconds. No chance even to think about the bunker. Just to press into the sandbags again and tremble, and tremble harder as one of the crashes, the loudest, is followed by the noise that dirt makes when it is thrown against the side of a tent. The tent shook and there was a quick tearing sound as a piece of steel, which turned out to be four inches long, an inch wide, half an inch thick, and jagged, ripped through the canvas of the tent. Then, for a moment, silence.

Joe Stringfield stuck his head up. "Let's go!" He grabbed his helmet, shoved it on top of his head, and, shirtless, and wearing only socks on his feet, he raced, crouching, through the flaps of the tent and toward the bunker, which was less than thirty yards away. The bunker was dug about four feet into the ground and there were another two feet of sandbags piled up around the sides and a heavy ceiling of sandbags across the top. Three orange dots began to dance in the dark and the breathing was very heavy. The whispers kept coming, and the crashes, and Joe Stringfield shook his head. "Sonofabitch. I knew we were overdue."

After fifteen minutes, the whispers stopped. After another five minutes, Joe Stringfield stuck his head above the entrance to the bunker. "I think it's all right now. I'd better check my men for casualties."

Then it came again. WhisperCRASH! Whisper-CRASH! And Joe Stringfield ducked back into the hole in the ground.

I went to see the colonel. It was 3:15 a.m. He was eating scrambled eggs and drinking coffee. The colonel was going to lead the patrol.

"Morning," he said. "Grab some chow."

"Good morning, colonel."

"Hope the noise of that mortar didn't disturb your sleep."

"Well, a little."

"We were lucky. Very lucky. Only one wounded in the whole camp. Charlie Company up the road a few clicks reported two killed and five wounded. And Dogface, down below us, is still being hit. Well, better hurry and eat. And then go back to String-field. He'll outfit you. Steel pot, flak jacket, and you'd better carry a rifle. Ever used one before?"

"Colonel?"

"Yes?" I had played volleyball with him the previous evening, and had sat with him in his tent, after dark, listening to him talk about his family.

"I'm not going on the patrol."

"I beg your pardon?"

"I said I won't be going on the patrol."

"What do you mean? Why not?"

"I've . . . I've just decided not to."

"I don't understand."

"I . . . I just think I'd rather stay here."

"Yesterday you told me you wanted to go on this patrol."

"I know. But I've changed my mind."

The colonel had pale gray eyes. He looked straight at me. "Have you ever been on a night patrol?"

"No, sir."

"Ever seen incoming mortar before last night?"

"No, sir."

He looked at me for several seconds without speaking. Then he said: "I think you'd be better off, son, if you came on this patrol."

I hesitated. Then I said: "I just don't want to."

"You're sure of that?"

"Yes, sir."

He did not look at me any more. "All right," he said. "We'll provide you with transportation out of here later in the day. Now if you'll excuse me . . ."

"Of course."

I left the mess tent. I went back to my own tent and lay there as the patrol went into the woods. I lay in the tent with my eyes open until dawn.

I wanted very much to see Ted Kennedy. I wanted to get close to him, see what he saw, feel what he felt. I wanted him to get drunk with me and tell me what it was like to be him. I wanted to know him the way I had hoped to know his brother. I wanted to experience his myth, since I finally had been able to admit to myself that I would not have one of my own. I called his press secretary. I said I was writing a book about my search for the vanished American hero. I said I wanted to spend some time with Senator Kennedy.

"I don't think so," the press secretary said.

"You don't think so?"

"I don't think I could recommend that to the senator."

"Why not?"

"Frankly, I'm not sure we could trust you."

"What do you mean?"

"Look, the senator is very open. He's a very candid guy. People around here who write about him understand this. They play by a certain set of rules. But you're a one-shot artist, coming in from outside. And, as I understand it, you play by a different set of rules."

"I'm not sure I know what you mean."

"Say you're on a trip with him. Say you're sitting with him on the way back, on the plane. Say you're on your way back from Spokane. And he says, just in conversation, that the mayor of Spokane is an asshole. Now, that's just an example. I don't think actually he even knows the mayor of Spokane. One of the regular guys would know enough not to print that. With a guy like you, we couldn't be sure."

I had to talk to the press secretary, off and on, for several weeks. I had to fly to Washington to talk to him in person. I had to have friends of mine who knew him talk to him. Finally, he said it would be all right for me to see the senator. I could come to Washington and spend a week around the office. Later, I could go with the senator when he made an out-of-town trip. Presumably, not to Spokane.

But the press secretary gave me a warning: "This hero business is one thing he gets uptight about. I don't know how you can work it, but when you're explaining about your book you'd be much better off if you downplayed that angle. It makes him uncomfortable as hell to have people come in and want to talk about the Kennedy mystique or the myth of the Kennedys or the Kennedys as heroes, that sort of thing. That's something he just doesn't like to deal with. I've seen it happen so many times in the past: things are going fine, he's very loose and relaxed, and then somebody brings up that Kennedy-legend stuff, or asks him something about Camelot or carrying the torch, and he freezes. He absolutely freezes. His eyes glaze over and that muscle on the right side of his face starts to twitch and then it's all over, buddy. He pulls back into his shell and you've had it."

I saw Ted Kennedy, at noon, in his office. He looked heavy and tired. His wife was in a rest home where alcoholism was treated. His son had just had a leg cut off because of cancer. Mary Jo Kopechne had drowned at Chappaquiddick. His three brothers were dead, two of them murdered. His own back had been broken in a plane crash. And now he was expected to run for President.

He said he did not understand what I wanted. I said I was writing a book and that I wanted to put him in the book. I said I wanted to spend some time with him and get to know him. He nodded. Everybody wanted something. I was perspiring. I wished that we were having this talk over a drink instead of on little chairs in a corner of his office. I wished that it was 1967 and that I was talking to his brother instead of to him.

"Tell me about the book," he said.

"Well, it's sort of a book about the hero in America and what's happened to him and why we don't seem to have heroes any more the way we used to."

He looked at me intently and said nothing. I smiled.

"I mean, well, you know, it's sort of going to be like a book about my search for the vanished American hero."

He continued to look at me intently, saying nothing.

"Now of course I realize that this isn't a subject we can really talk about at great length, because I know how . . . well, how it's just, ah, kind of hard to talk about." I smiled. "But you see, it seems to me that this kind of book—and now I'm not trying to make you uncomfortable—but that there really would have to be something about the Kennedys, and I mean about yourself in particular, in this kind of book."

He was still staring. Waiting.

"You know, everybody says we don't have heroes any more, but, on the other hand, there is this special sort of feeling that people have about the Kennedys. About, you know, the whole Kennedy thing. That's why I'd like to spend a little time with you."

I was perspiring more heavily. There was so much of him which had been buried for the sake of the legend. What was it costing him, and how aware was he of the cost? Which of his illusions had survived? How tightly did he cling to them? What would happen if he let go? I wanted to know what it was like down there. As Adrienne Rich had written: *"I came to explore the wreck . . . the wreck and not the story of the wreck. The thing itself and not the myth."*

"Look, five years ago everybody thought your brother was a hero. Including me. I spent a little time with him that spring. I wrote about him. In fact, I was up in the hospital where he died. And now, see, there's all that feeling floating around out there loose and you seem to be the only one it can focus on."

He was still staring. But not, it seemed, quite so intently.

"What I'd really like to do, you see, is just spend some time with you. Not actually talking about things like this, but, well, you know, just sort of hanging around."

He was still looking at me. But now not intently at all. In fact, his eyes seemed glazed. He remained silent. Then a muscle on the right side of his face began to twitch.

J 1970

JANUARY   My book was number one. Great to be
young and a Yankee. I came to town to do the Cavett
show and I threw a party in my suite at the
Warwick. Six months earlier, I had lain in front of a
television set with my wife, watching the Cavett
show, and it had seemed another world, light-years
away. She had said maybe someday you'll be on it,
and I had said oh, don't be silly, and I'd meant it.
Now I had done Cavett, Carson, Griffin, and all the
rest. I had debated the House minority leader,
Gerald Ford, on the David Frost show, and, quite
clearly, he had come out second best. Back home,
the Democratic organization in my county had
asked me to run for Congress. But I was too busy
having fun. Nancy came to the party. I had not seen
her before. Toward dawn, everyone went home.
Leaving behind stale smoke, stained rugs, over-
turned furniture, broken glass. Nancy stayed. We
ate room-service breakfast amid the debris. Fresh
sunlight streamed through yellow curtains. It

seemed we were the only two survivors of a holocaust. Nancy wore my undershirt to the table. It turned out that she worked for my publisher. We held hands and gazed dumbly across the table at each other. There was FM music on the radio. It was love.

FEBRUARY   I met her at the airport on a Friday night. This was my third trip to Los Angeles in two months. We flew first-class and drank everything they gave us and asked for more. Already, I was needing help with my illusions. People met us at the airport in Los Angeles with champagne. They wanted to talk to me about making a movie from my book. A boat was hired and lots of us went to Catalina for the day. Nancy and I lay by ourselves across the bow, holding hands. On the way back the boat's engine broke down. We were ferried back to Catalina and spent the night. It was romantic. Like a honeymoon. Except I had to leave the table during dinner to call my wife. Then the sun rose and our plane landed and we were east again without sleep, in New York at six-thirty on a winter work-morning. We stumbled down the ramp into an experimental telephone booth called a Chatterbox. It was big enough for six people to sit down in at once. There was no receiver, only a dial on the wall. You talked into an empty space and the voice of the person to whom you were talking came to you from out of the walls all around you. We called lots of my friends and woke them up. Just so Nancy could say hello. We had been drinking Irish whisky on the plane. It was fun at first, but then it got scary, sitting in an empty glass box, talking at the walls, and not having anything to hold on to. Nancy rode with me on the train to Philadelphia. Then she went back to New York. I took a cab home and went to bed. I woke up in late afternoon. My wife wanted to know if I had been with a girl in California. I said yes.

MARCH   I went to London for the publication of the British edition of my book. My wife went with me. I told her I would be leaving her when we got back. We stayed a week. Then we flew home and my wife's father met us at the airport with our daughters. Our daughter was three and a half. The other was about to be two. Then my wife told me she was pregnant. The new baby was due in October. Great to be young and a Yankee. Not so great to be young and a Yankee's wife.

APRIL   I rented a house that stood alone on a hillside at the northwest edge of New Jersey. The Delaware River flowed a quarter mile below. The nearest town was nine miles south. The house was four-stories high and contained twenty-one rooms. It had been built as a resort hotel in the late 1800s. There was a wide porch and a view of the river and of Pennsylvania hills. Only four rooms were open and heated. The rest was a great, dark, empty, creaking cavern. Nancy came out on weekends and Wednesday nights. We laughed all the time in the beginning. At quarter to six on work-mornings, when the alarm went off in the dark. "Are you sure," she asked, "that I'm not just a passing Nancy?" When she was not there I did not laugh.

MAY   And warm mellow weekends. Nancy's two teen-age sisters came to visit. And brought another girl along. The five of us swam naked in the river. We traveled a lot: to the Caribbean, to the Kentucky Derby, to speeches I was making around the country. Then we came back and gave a party. We opened up the whole house and gave a party for sixty people on the weekend of the Preakness. It was marvelous. I was Gatsby. And the rest of my life would be a party. Except that my wife called often on the phone. She pleaded with me to return. There were long, stuttering silences filled with sorrow. And my mother called, and my father, and pleaded, too. And my dreams were bad. I dreamed of going back to my wife and finding her old and horribly wrinkled. And I dreamed terrible dreams about the maiming and destruction of my daughters.

SUMMER We moved to Roxbury and began to live together all the time. Nancy commuted to her job in New York. I started working on a novel. We had wine in the evenings and fires on damp nights. On weekends the mountains were dancing. I played a lot of tennis on Styron's court. Arthur Miller was a frequent doubles partner. One day I had lunch with my father in the city. He seemed old and sad and under strain. He took several sheets of folded yellow paper from his pocket. He said that the night before he and my mother had prepared a list of the reasons why I should return to my wife. He read from the list like a representative of management in a labor negotiation. I told him I would take his arguments under advisement.

SEPTEMBER I went out to buy tennis balls. I stopped at a stop sign. I saw a blue car with

Massachusetts license plates. My wife's parents were in the car. They had come to Roxbury to talk to me. They came to the house. They thought I was living there alone. They talked to me for more than an hour. As Nancy lay silently on a bed one floor above.

OCTOBER The baby was born. I went to the delivery room and held my wife's hand as she gave birth. It was a boy. My wife cried, "Thank God!" For five days I visited her and the baby in the hospital and slept in the house with my daughters. Then I brought my wife and baby home. The next morning, I went away again.

NOVEMBER Nancy and I were living in New Jersey, near where I had lived in the spring. She had quit her job and was with me all the time. The paperback edition of my book was number one. I still went around the country making speeches. At Harvard, in Houston, anywhere that would get my mind off my own life. I tried to work on my novel when I was home. I spent Thanksgiving with my children and my wife. My parents were there, feeling sad. Everyone paid a lot of attention to the baby.

DECEMBER My birthday. I was twenty-eight. The year-end edition of *Playboy* was published, containing interviews with nine authors "who have scored with the bitch goddess of fame." Mario Puzo, James Dickey, Kurt Vonnegut, Studs Terkel, Michael Crichton, Sam Houston Johnson, Dan Wakefield, Gay Talese, and myself. Great to be young and a Yankee. Except I lay awake, trembling, every night.

I went to Massachusetts. Ted Kennedy had said I could follow him around as he traveled throughout the state during Senate recess. He was making a dozen public appearances a day. He would start at breakfast, sometimes before, and continue late into the night—being seen, heard, touched, being experienced. Renewing the legend at its roots. He was moving, always moving: Quincy, Weymouth, Hingham, New Bedford, Fall River, Framingham, Worcester, Palmer, Springfield, Holyoke, Lowell, Lawrence, Everett, Tewkesbury, Peabody, Malden, Waltham. For six days, he caromed around the state like a pinball.

It was a campaign atmosphere without a campaign. (Except for the constant campaign to breathe new life, pump new blood, into the myth.) Before and after each appearance there was a great milling and rushing of aides. Instructions were shouted, doors were slammed, cars were shifted frantically into reverse, U-turns were made on busy streets, speed limits were exceeded, traffic lights, bad weather, hunger pangs were ignored. It seemed a fire drill: just in case. It did not seem to matter that there was no opponent, no purpose to it all. This was the way Jack had done it and this was the way Bobby had done it and this was the way Teddy was going to do it. There would not be any slippage. The torch had to be carried and the torch had to be carried *fast*.

On four of the six days he was accompanied by his nephew Joe, who was Robert Kennedy's oldest son. On the sixth day, he was accompanied also by Caroline, daughter of John, and Courtney, daughter of Robert. For one day, he was joined by a Sargent Shriver son, and, on the final evening, by Kathleen, daughter of Robert, and her husband. And, each day, he seemed to be accompanied also by members of his family who were not present.

He went to the cafeteria of the Sacred Heart School in North Quincy. A low-ceilinged building, smoky and hot, and jammed with the adoring women of the parish. He said: "I'd like you to say hello to my nephew Joe." The young man, who was friendly and who had long, tangled hair, stood, grinned shyly, and gave a little wave. The women of the Sacred Heart shrieked with joy. *The nephew! Bobby's boy!* Cheering, applause, flash cubes, Instamatics. "Joe says he's not going to get his hair cut until I get re-elected." Laughter, more cheering, more applause. This was more than they had bargained for. This truly, was new blood. This was— imagine it!—the start of a *whole new generation*.

Then Ted Kennedy talked about his son. And about his son's recovery from amputation. He told an anecdote: after the operation, his son had received a football from the New England Patriots, a basketball from the Celtics, a baseball from the Red Sox, and a hockey stick from the Boston Bruins. And had said: "I know I have to learn sports again, Daddy, but do I have to learn them all at once?" It was an anecdote that Ted Kennedy told publicly six times a day.

He went to Holyoke High School. Joe Kennedy went with him. The school band played. Female students jumped and shrieked. Joe Kennedy was introduced. Pandemonium. He might as well have been a Rolling Stone. Then Ted Kennedy was given a Holyoke High School letter-sweater for his son. He told the anecdote about the sports equipment in response. Snow fell heavily and piled up outside. Other schools, and offices, had been shut. The roads were becoming impassable. It did not matter. The show must go on.

He went to the Springfield Young Democrats Club. Joe Kennedy went with him. The hall was crowded, smoky and hot. He arrived at eight-thirty, an hour late. There was frenzied cheering and loud Irish music. Consumption of alcohol on the premises was not forbidden. Ted Kennedy said to the crowd: "This is the biggest gathering of young Democrats I've been to since last Saturday, when I had dinner at Ethel's house." A huge picture of Robert Kennedy hung overhead. There was a speech about Robert Kennedy by Mayor Sullivan: "None of us will ever forget Robert Kennedy . . . seems like only yesterday . . . touch football on the lawn . . . dedicated himself to youthful ideals . . . man of deep compassion . . . none of us can ever forget . . . wished to seek a newer world . . . dreamed things that never were, and said why not . . . ." Then Mayor Sullivan spoke about the spirit of the Kennedy brothers: "The spirit of the Kennedy brothers emanates. . . . The spirit of the Kennedy brothers is a source of inspiration. . . ." Then Ted Kennedy was given a painting of Robert Kennedy. It had been done by a local artist who was almost totally paralyzed. Who "only had the use of a couple of fingers on one hand." Kennedy took the picture, looked at it, expressionless, and passed it on to an aide. Later, Joe Kennedy was made to dance a jig.

He went to Saint Mary's High School in Westfield. The introduction was made by Father O'Connor. Father O'Connor spoke of "two beautiful women, Mrs. Rose Kennedy and Mrs. Joan Kennedy." Then Father O'Connor told a story about how once he had sat on a dais with Joan Kennedy at a time when "that beautiful woman was very, very, very much expecting." Father O'Connor recalled having been "very impressed by the very beautiful and radiant Mrs. Joan Kennedy." Then, taking note of the fact that Ted Kennedy had arrived one hour late, Father O'Connor concluded: "I don't know what Senator Kennedy has going for him—besides tardiness—except a very wonderful mother and a very beautiful and radiant wife."

He went to the New Bedford High School auditorium. Joe Kennedy went with him. A song was performed in their honor. The song was "Abraham, Martin, and John," which had to do with the assassinations of Abraham Lincoln, Martin Luther King, and John and Robert Kennedy. . . .

He went to the office of a newspaper publisher. On the wall was a mat of the November 22, 1963, front page: PRES. KENNEDY IS DEAD. . . .

He went into a reception office at a high school. There was one book on a table. *John F. Kennedy: Words to Remember. With an Introductory Note by Robert F. Kennedy.*

He went to Fall River for ceremonies marking the induction into a nautical museum of the destroyer *Joseph P. Kennedy,* named for the first of his brothers to die. . . .

He went to a New Bedford supermarket to discuss high prices with shoppers. He was approached by an old man. "Now don't you do like your brother and—like your two brothers did. We need you alive. . . ."

He went to the Springfield Golden Age Club. Joe Kennedy went with him. Two old ladies watched them pass.

First old lady: "That one there. Is he one of them, too?"

Second old lady: "Yes, that's the nephew. You can tell he's one of them when he smiles. You can always tell them by their smiles."

I approached him one night after dinner. I said: "Senator, I know you've been busy for these three days and we haven't had much chance to talk, but I hope that when you come back next week we will."

"It's hard to tell," he said. "I keep a pretty full schedule up here." I thought of what the Philadelphia columnist Sandy Grady had once written: that he was "stuck in time, like a fly in amber." And that he was "distant, as if behind glass."

"Well, I'll see you next week anyway. I'm coming back up."

"You think you can stand another three days?"

"Oh, sure. This is interesting."

There seemed a sudden flash of curiosity. He said, "It is?"

"Well. At least as much for me as it is for you."

He laughed. Spontaneously. It was the only moment of contact we ever had.

T he phone rings. My 7:00-a.m. wake-up call from the desk. But I am already awake. I have been awake a long time. I get up and take a long, hot, soapy shower. On this day, of all days, it is important to be clean. I eat breakfast in the coffee shop with my mother and father. Then I come back to my room and dress in my rented formal suit. There are a lot of buttons and the cuff links don't fit and it is hard to get my tie tied right. My father helps me. Then he takes pictures. Then, with my best man, a friend from high school, I drive four miles up the road to Pittsfield, and the church. It is September 25, 1965, and still warm in the Berkshires. The ceremony will begin at eleven. . . .

I had met her in May, a year earlier, just before I graduated from Holy Cross. It was a weekend, and, as usual, there weren't any girls around, and somebody said he knew a girl in a nursing school down in Hartford and he called her and she said she had a couple of friends who weren't doing anything so we drove down there and I spent the next four or five hours in a car parked outside the motel room we had rented for the party, listening to Bobby Vee sing "Rubber Ball" ("Like a rubber ball, I come bouncing back to you-hoo-hoo") and telling this cute little blond girl the story of my life. The next night I drove back to Hartford by myself and she handed me a pink rubber ball she had bought and I told her all about my ambitions for the future. By September I had a job on the Worcester *Telegram* and her nursing school sent her to Worcester for two months of special training. One Sunday in November I drove to Pittsfield and met her parents and had dinner at their house. Her father worked at the General Electric plant. Her mother fed me mashed potatoes and suspicious glances. By Christmas, we were engaged. She was cheerful and tender and unselfish and a good Catholic. She thought I was wonderful and she wanted to help me become a great writer. I loved her so much I thought I would burst. I had always been lonely, and so had she, and now we would not be lonely any more.

We left the reception in late afternoon. It had been overcast but now the sun shone brilliantly and the air was fresh and mountain-cool. We were going to New York. My father had got us a suite at the Essex House for the weekend. Then we were going to go somewhere else for a few days. Then I would go back to my new job as a sports writer for the Philadelphia *Bulletin* and we would move into our cozy new apartment in the suburbs, with our Sears dinette set and our new double bed, the very thought of which excited me.

The sun was low in the sky and there were hints of autumn along the Taconic State Parkway as I drove. I looked at my wedding ring, shiny and unfamiliar. It made me feel proud. And grown-up. The sun shone into the car from the right. I looked in that direction and saw tears in my wife's eyes. She was beautiful and I loved her and I did not want her ever to cry. I asked what was wrong. She said it was nothing: she just felt a little afraid. About tonight? I asked. About our wedding night? You don't have to be afraid. There's no hurry. I won't rush. She said no, that was not it. She said she was just a little afraid about the future. About this new life I was taking her to, so far from anyone and anything she'd ever known, with only my promises as her guide.

I told her she had nothing to fear. I told her I loved her and always would and that as long as she had that to depend on there was nothing of which she would have to be afraid. She said she knew that. She said she knew she was just being silly. She said probably she was overly emotional at the moment, due to all the excitement. I said yes, that was it. She would feel better in a little while. I put my arm around her. She slid close to me on the seat. Off to our right, the sun set.

And here is the last thing I did: I went to the Test Pilot School at Edwards Air Force Base in Lancaster, California. I went there because I had begun to sense that I had no more to find in restaurants, or offices, or in the living rooms of the renowned. No more to gain by continuing to chase after the famous. They already had their illusions. I still was searching for mine.

I went to the Test Pilot School because it seemed to me that the men there—instructors and students —provided as vivid an affirmation as was possible of the existence of satisfactory illusions. Test pilots were not necessarily American heroes, but they were men who believed—and who, every day, staked their life on their belief—in the wildest, most improbable of illusions: that they belonged in the air and not on the ground. This illusion sustained them, rewarded them, filled up their lives. Or else it killed them. "Death Is the Greatest Kick of All" a sign at the Test Pilot School said, "That's Why They Save It for Last."

I stayed overnight at the home of an instructor. He was a graying, soft-spoken, thirty-five-year-old major from Darien, Connecticut, named Fred Porter. Of the twelve men who had comprised his first squadron, in 1967, only he and one other were still alive. But Fred Porter, with a wife and two small children, flew every day. He said he did not think that death was the greatest kick of all: he said it was hard to imagine that anything could beat flying.

So one morning I put on a flight suit and helmet and oxygen mask and a pack that contained a parachute, and I rode out to the flight line and climbed into the rear cockpit of one of the jet planes that are used to teach regular military pilots how to become test pilots. An instructor from the Test Pilot School climbed into the front cockpit. He explained to me what all the buttons and dials were for, and then he explained very carefully about how to work the ejection seat. I did not tell him I was afraid of high places. Or that I was afraid to ride roller coasters, or even ferris wheels, at amusement parks.

He got clearance from the tower and started the engines and began to taxi toward the runway. The plane bounced. It was a small, white plane, shaped like a dart. We got to the runway. I lowered the canopy over my cockpit and locked it into place. It had been a warm, clear spring day in the desert. Now it was hot. All sound was cut off, except for my breathing into the oxygen mask and whatever the pilot said to me through my earphones. I felt cramped. My helmet was uncomfortable. I was starting to perspire.

Then the pilot got the clearance he was waiting for. We were off. Rushing, bumping crazily down the runway. Then we were up. No more bumping. Instead, the push of gravity, forcing me down into my seat. Blue overhead, then blue all around. The gravity-pressure eased. It wasn't so bad. Nice and smooth. Then the pilot said something about "afterburner" and there was a low roaring sound and I was pushed back into the seat again and we were climbing like a fly climbs a wall.

We flew across the desert to snow-covered mountains and dove low over the summits of the highest. Always before, in the Rockies, in the Alps, I had been low on the mountain looking up. Now I was at the top looking down. Mountains for miles. For hundreds of miles. Covered with snow. We dove, and leveled off seventy-five feet above the desert floor. Then we headed for the base for what was called a "tower fly-by." This is where the pilot flies in front of the control tower at four hundred and fifty miles an hour, while trying to hold the plane on a perfect horizontal course as close to the ground as possible. It is a standard exercise, sort of a calisthenic, at the Test Pilot School. We did it twice. The first time, I closed my eyes. The second time, I kept them open.

Then we went up again and rolled and spun and climbed and dove and flew faster than sound. It was like riding on the feathers of an arrow. Then the pilot said: "You fly it."

I took the stick in my hands and clumsily, cautiously, fearfully, began to control the movement of the plane.

"Don't be afraid of it. It won't bite."

After a few minutes the pilot said: "Okay. Now roll it."

And without even thinking about it because if I thought about it I would have been too afraid to do it, I pulled the stick to the left and kept pulling and pulling and the plane tipped and tipped and kept tipping and I felt like I was going to fall out and I wanted to stop but I kept going more and more and then the ground was above me and the sky below and then the sky was above and the ground below and then ground again, then sky, spinning faster and faster as I sat still (it seemed) and over and over we rolled into the blue and I had the stick in my hand and all this time we were going faster than sound *and I had the stick in my hand.*

Joseph Campbell wrote:

The mythological hero, setting forth from his commonday hut or castle, is lured, carried away, or else voluntarily proceeds, to the threshold of adventure. There he encounters a shadow presence that guards the passage. The hero may defeat or conciliate this power and go alive into the kingdom of the dark, or be slain by the opponent and descend in death. Beyond the threshold, then, the hero journeys through a world of unfamiliar yet strangely intimate forces, some of which severely threaten him, some of which give magical aid. When he arrives at the nadir of the mythological round, he undergoes a supreme ordeal and gains his reward. The triumph may be represented as the hero's sexual union with the goddess-mother of the world, his recognition by the father-creator, his own divinization, or again—if the powers have remained unfriendly to him—his theft of the boon he came to gain; intrinsically, it is an expansion of consciousness and therewith of being. The final work is that of the return. If the powers have blessed the hero he now sets forth under their protection; if not, he flees and is pursued. At the return threshold the transcendental powers must remain behind; the hero re-emerges from the kingdom of dread. . . .

Richard Nixon is walking across a flat and arid landscape. In the distance there is a low, boxlike building without windows. A hospital. Richard Nixon is surrounded by pushing, shoving, television crews, and by dozens of reporters as he walks. He is speaking in a quiet, controlled voice. There is a slight smile on his face. Richard Nixon has a brain tumor. He is walking across the flat, arid land to the hospital where an operation will be performed. Richard Nixon knows the operation will not succeed. He knows that he will not regain consciousness when it is over. He is telling all this to the reporters as he walks. He walks steadily, not in a hurry, but not showing fear. This is his last press conference. It really is. . . .

I have other dreams. I dream that my father is alive. I am with him. But he is very cold and I can find no way to make him warm. There are long, awkward silences. We cannot find much to say to each other. What I want—desperately—is to ask him what it is like to be dead. But there is a rule against that. It is part of the arrangement whereby he is alive. He can only remain alive so long as he does not talk about what it was like to be dead. . . .

One night I had a different kind of dream. I dreamed that a flying saucer landed near my house. Thousands of people had gathered. It was determined that I was to go aboard the flying saucer. No one else. Not Nancy, not my wife, not my mother, not my children, not my friends. Only me. I did not know why I had been selected. The flying saucer would take me away. The journey would be long, and the most terrifying I had ever known. For what seemed light-years I would have to sit on the edge of the flying saucer: open, unprotected, exposed. I would be terribly, terribly afraid that I would fall. Off the edge. Out into dark endless space. My fear would become so great that there was danger I would jump, simply to end it. But I knew—and this filled me with elation—that if I could stand it, if I did not jump, if I could force myself to stay with it until the end—I would arrive in a new dimension beyond dimensions, in a new galaxy of pure joy. I did not know how long I would remain there. I did not know if I ever would come back. It did not matter. Knowing that this new dimension existed, and that I was bound there, was enough. It suffused me with color and light, like a rainbow; filled me with infinity, like a god.

It is July 8, 1975. I spoke to my mother today. She is living alone in the house in Rye. She does not go out much. She does not go to church any more. She does not believe any longer that people go to heaven when they die.

On this day, thirty-six years ago, my mother and father were married. Not long ago I looked at movies of the wedding. My mother had dark hair and seemed excited. I do not remember her as ever having had anything but gray hair. But there, in the movies, it was dark. My father looked tall and awkward and unsure of himself. The same way I looked in pictures taken on my wedding day.

My search is over. At least for now. And, as I guess you have surmised, I did not find any heroes. At least not of the kind I was looking for. No one who "provided a transcendental link between the contingencies of the finite and the imagined realm of the supernatural." No one who, as critic Ihab Hassan put it, "unites the course of history and the stream of dreams." Perhaps Mailer was right when he wrote: "There is only a modern hero, damned by no more than the ugliness of wishes whose satisfaction he will never know."

But maybe not. One night I had dinner with Joseph Campbell. He said he thought that in America today we were at a point which corresponded to the point in Indian history, thousands of years ago, at which the word for "hero" was just beginning to change its meaning. Up to that point, Campbell said, the Indian word for "hero" could be translated as "warrior." Beyond that point, the proper translation became "prophet."

In *The Hero with a Thousand Faces*, published more than twenty years ago, Campbell wrote: "The hero deed to be wrought is not today what it was in the century of Galileo. Where then there was darkness, now there is light; but also, where light was, there now is darkness. The modern hero-deed must be that of questing to bring to light again the lost Atlantis of the coordinated soul. . . .

"The problem is nothing if not that of rendering the modern world spiritually significant—or rather —nothing if not that of making it possible for men and women to come to full human maturity through the conditions of contemporary life."

I do not know of anyone who has done that for us in the past twenty years, or who is about to do that for us today. There may be those, however, from time to time, who will give us help in little ways. Who will do what Pete Hamill said Bob Dylan did in the sixties. "When our innocence died," Hamill wrote, "Bob Dylan made that moment into art."

Mostly, however, I think we will have to get by for

a while with private symbols. I do not think we can be as comfortable as we once were with hand-me-down illusions; with prefabricated myths. I think, as Campbell has suggested, that each of us who seeks dimension will have to construct his own mosaic; will have to build his own myth, slowly, painfully, piece by piece.

I am busy now, working on mine. Actually, I do not think it will turn out to be anything so grand as a myth. At best, it is likely to be no more than a temporarily useful illusion.

Such as: that writing about an experience, or life, can give it meaning. That writing about the loss of illusions—the vanishing of heroes—can compensate, in however small and unsatisfactory a way, for the no longer deniable fact that they are gone.

EPILOGUE

Fourteen years have passed since *Heroes* was originally published. For its author, they have been better ones than the book might have led a reader to expect. I have not constructed any myths of lasting value that I'm aware of, and even at forty-six I am reluctant to claim "full human maturity," but the publication of three subsequent books—*Going to Extremes*, *Fatal Vision, and Blind Faith*—has, at least, added to my mosaic. Also, certain aspects of my personal life have turned out to be more than "temporarily useful illusions."

Nancy and I married in 1976. We have two sons, aged eleven and six. My three older children have grown into splendid young adults, a fact for which their mother deserves great credit. Chris, the oldest, graduated from Boston College in 1988. Suzi is a junior at Widener University. Joe is a freshman at Swarthmore.

Of those public figures upon whose generosity I presumed during the peculiar quest described herein, many have continued to flourish. With a few, such as William Styron, Arthur Miller and Howard Cosell, I've maintained cordial, if occasional, contact. I remain especially in the debt of William F. Buckley, who, at considerable inconvenience to himself, testified in my behalf during the 1987 trial of a lawsuit arising from the publication of *Fatal Vision*.

George McGovern and Eugene McCarthy have retired from politics, while John Glenn and Edward Kennedy remain active. (Kennedy, who still seems to me to be the one contemporary American public figure whose life has been equally intersected by history and myth, will be the subject of my next book.)

To the best of my knowledge, as of this writing, Daniel Berrigan, still a Jesuit, resides in New York City. William Westmoreland is living in retirement in South Carolina. Secretariat (whose equal has not been seen since) died last fall at the age of nineteen. About Joe Hooper, Tim Sullivan and Fred Porter, I can report nothing.

Through a series of remarkable television interviews conducted by Bill Moyers, Joseph Campbell, who died last year, finally reached the wide audience to which his provocative and ennobling ideas entitled him. As our journey toward "x" continues, his writings remain as reliable a guide as we're likely to find.

Joe McGinniss
Williamstown, Mass.
February 1990